D1739270

THE
LEAFLESS AMERICAN

BY EDWARD DAHLBERG

Edited and With an Introduction
By Harold Billings

ROGER BEACHAM • PUBLISHER

WITHDRAWN
Pierce Library
Eastern Oregon University
From EOU Library
1410 L Avenue
La Grande, OR 97850

Copyright © 1967 by Edward Dahlberg

Designed by Barbara Holman

With grateful acknowledgments to Francis Brown, Book Editor, of the *New York Times Book Review,* for permission to reprint "The Malice of Witlings"; to Jonathan Williams, Publisher, for "Mid-American Chants: Sherwood Anderson"; and to the Humanities Research Center of The University of Texas for access to manuscript sources.

CONTENTS

Introduction   vii

The Leafless American   1

A Decline of Souls   6

Kansas City Revisited   17

Tears of the Virgin   27

Rome and America   38

How Do You Spell Fool   41

The Malice of Witlings   49

Stephen Crane: American Genius   58

Mid-American Chants: Sherwood Anderson   62

Oscar Wilde : The Sin of Paradox   65

The True Nietzsche   69

Methuselah's Funeral   75

The Garment of Rā   81

The Sandals of Judith   97

INTRODUCTION

Edward Dahlberg has had a slow-growing but hardy, oaken reputation. Blessed and burdened with one of the great voices in American literature he has long likened himself to Ishmael and Job and lived an eremitic life of writing, caring only to please himself. His circle of admirers includes many of the finest writers and he has been gratuitously imitated, but he spent forty years in the wilderness of critical neglect. *Because I Was Flesh*, which may prove to be the finest prose work ever composed by a twentieth-century American, brought him to the attention of many new admirers. This book and *The Flea of Sodom, Can These Bones Live*, and *The Sorrows of Priapus* have firmly rooted him in the living earth of our letters. At an age when most men have framed the few laurels luck has brought them, Dahlberg works away at the height of his lyrical, creative maturity.

Dahlberg's words are shaped in a matrix of winds from the four geographic corners of his sensibility: the Hellenic, the Hebraic, the American primitive-pastoral, and what he would perhaps term his own personal "Pulse." Style and man are one. Dahlberg is a moralist. He feels we cannot know our present and can only hope to shape a puissant future by turning to the past, to our ancestors, to the great mythographers of man's spirit, to the geographers of our oceans and forests, for polestars of style and the perdurable values by which man must live.

For style and form, then, he turns to the great Greek and Hebraic writers, their heirs the Elizabethans, and to the chroniclers of early America. Each of his books is a love-child, the result of a pillage into some classic beauty. He has said in a poem, "Let me, O Heaven, pluck her green virginity"; he could as easily be speaking of an ancient work of art as he is the Universe, a haw, or a maiden.

All great prose stylists are only a jot away from poetry. This is particularly true of Dahlberg. His writing moves in classical, biblical cadence; every aphoristic line is black-letter verse. This is style from the oldest fonts of song. But his facile pen is not caught solely in the rich calligraphy of savory Elizabethan style; he varies his approach to suit his subject. Thus, he can essay on locale with easy, journalistic evocativeness, or produce a prophetic poem as compressed and brilliant as opal ore. This is the mark of rare artistry.

His values follow closely those ancient laws of Israel that prescribe justice, familial honor, and humility. In all his writing can be seen the pendulum swing of the head and heart of the Judaic prophets: the earth was created for man but man must again become part of that earth. Man sings high but must go low; he erects his manhood, then grovels in the dust. Dahlberg remains a flea in our modern Sodom. He is an angry American Moses casting down the tables from a cordilleran Sinai. He reviles the brazen Machine. He psalms of the grape, the potato, a coat button, but he does it with a complexity that might often shame the most postured academic idol. And there is a vision beyond each opacity. The reader must ascend to Dahlberg and acclimate to the mists and mountains of his altitude. He makes no concessions.

Dahlberg often sings of sex but decries lewdness. His muse is an intellectual Eros. His Adam and Eve discard the mythic fig-leaf for a Word and bury the fig in the heart. Dahlberg pleads for acceptance of carnal woman in our literature, for jocund flesh and food, for all the fertile streams and seed buried by the ice-age of Puritanism.

Perhaps no American writer since Thoreau has been so enamoured of our natural history, our woodlands, meadows, rivers, and their creatures. These are the gardens we left for lucre's apple. For Dahlberg every rock is a relic and a day-break rooster heritages in his heart; the Mississippi is a Nile and Leviathan slumbers in its mud; our ancestors' blood and bone are dew and compost from which the wild plum grows. Man and his frailties are simply a part of the great cycle of the bloom and decay of civilization and flower.

The present collection brings together for the first time in book form various important pieces demonstrating Dahlberg's style, attitudes, and philosophy. The first and last are prose-poems cut from the brightest cloth of his thought and style, threads of which intertwine in all the other pieces. "The Leafless American" is a bit of his testament of American earth, a prayer for all our drifting seed-spirits to find root in some turf as the sycamore spores must if they are to renew themselves. "The Sandals of Judith," which closes the book, beats us low again with its reminder of man's sexual nature and mortality; after our years of flesh we cup the alms of quiet.

One of the major essays of Dahlberg's career is "A Decline of Souls," a commentary on the American social and economic state, the decline of pioneer energy into the Boot-hill of lassitude, the choice of no-choice between cartel and communism. Dahlberg digs the earth of his own past in "Kansas City Revisited"; "Tears of the Virgin" presents a picture of Spain seen through baroque eyes and comments on changing values. "Rome and America" steps farther back into a typical Dahlberg relativistic time period when Rome and America are made to sit side by side, sin by sin, in a harsh warning.

"How Do You Spell Fool?" offers a cogent commentary on reading and writing, and demonstrates as well the weakness of the modern critic who chips away at the physiognomy of writing but never charts its deep inner rivers. "The Malice of Witlings" is a similar acerb essay on the perverse criticaster who pins the poet to the cross of penury and neglect. The essays that follow show Dahlberg's own critical approach, his dialectical shaking of the surface of critical writing into a narcissistic pool that is revelatory not only of his subject but of the reader and his civilization as well.

"Methuselah's Funeral," an interesting experiment in style, combines a Cape Cod background with ancient animal worship and the bedlamite verse of eighteenth-century Christopher Smart. A rich exemplar of Dahlberg's most eloquent, compressed verse is "The Garment of Ra"; how finely expressive of the sterility of our wounded moment are its beginning lines:

The voice of the rains cannot find the rivers,
The leaves are orphaned by thrush and crane,
The hills cannot foal.

There is a lifetime of reading in this poem alone, for Dahlberg is so much, so complex, he cannot be reduced to explication. He can only be read, reread, and accepted as a writer unique, and uniquely American.

Long ago he gazed upon the open valley of our bleached letters and posed the question: Can these bones live? How can the bones of American literature help but live fleshed with writing such as his.

HAROLD BILLINGS

The University of Texas
September 10, 1966

x

THE LEAFLESS AMERICAN

THE LEAFLESS AMERICAN

How old are we?

We are still a horse and buffalo
people, heavy, lumbering cattle, with
prairie and grain virtues, and our avarice
is primitive wigwam barter; we ought to
adore the great fish god, for we are a
coastal people, and New Mexico and Arizona,
which are saurian undersea country, breeding
pine, cactus, and snakes, are Galilean land.

We are passing from a morning horse
innocence to unusual vices, and we are not
ready.

Is Pike's Peak a hummock of old world
sin, or the Rockies Scythian debauchery,
or the mineraled Colorado dawn the Orient
pearl? It is hay and brook and sweet pony
corral, appled meadow garnished with odors
more virtuous than spiced Eden.

Take no stock in American turpitudes;
look to the Toltec or the Mayan for the
lascivious parrot and monkey.

The Platte River, the pine, the sage
brush are hardy character, but not history,

1

and I admit that nothing has ever happened
to me, and that I am mad for events.

Whatever we do is vast, unconscious
geography; we are huge space giants of the
mesa, surd, mad rivers that rush along, and
we do not care to be near each other; this
is not ancient wickedness, but solitary
prairie grazing.

We cannot bear each other because we
are immense territory, and our most malignant
folly was to closet us up in cities, and take
away our ocean past .

We should have the deepest reverence
for poverty, because we are New Testament
ground. Every day I offer a sacrifice to
the extinct bison, the horse and savage
Iroquois, who are our muse of cereal, yam
and maize, and when somebody strokes my
head, I walk to Mt. Shasta, or the Oregon
orchards which are my epistles to the
Corinthians.

Who is my Father?

The rising sun-man has disappeared,
and the step-father, the petticoat parent,
is rearing the children since the tent,
the wagon, and saddle have gone.

The great, grassy basin, the Catskill
eagle made us tribal and fierce; the Pawnee,
leading the sorrel of the Platte by a bull-hide
rope, lessoned us in poverty, for want too
is a tough, rude god made out of dried buffalo
skin, to which we must offer our orisons, lest
we perish of sloth and surfeit.

Our forefathers were giant volcano-horses;
we were a hot earth animal as the elephant
shaped mounds found in Kansas show.

Give us back our origins, for I am out
of season in any other land, or plant except
the corn seeds of Quetzalcoatl, the yucca,
the cactus, and the Mojave joshua tree,
dearer than the desert tamarisk beneath
which Saul sat.

We have lost ground, city-cursed
that we are, left it behind us like the
Quiché did the Yaqui for whom they wept.

Return the Platte, the bison, the hoof-print
of the deer, for I am as hungry for them as
the wandering Quiché who had to smell the points
of their staffs to deceive their empty stomachs.

Our Mother paps were rabid gulches
in which the white and gray wolves howled,
and now that the Toltec and the Pawnee
are dead, we are their evil genius, looking
for a relic, a flint arrow, a tepee, a
harness, a piece of bread.

I need confidence, the antelope, the
pack-mule, the Indian apple, but we have
killed the old bread gods made of plums,
incense and the coca plant. Until we find
the Quiché bread idol, we are orphans.

The word together has become a tabu
devil; everything is public except guilt,
which is hidden like hands that are pursed
and pocketed lest they be demanded for
hand-shaking, which is some uneasy, first
sin; touch a man and the blood goes out
of his cheek; the mountains, the hills and
the grass are turning against men, and
every man dreads every man.

The mating season that once cattled
the fingers of the marriageable now brings
the alley tree, cemented in the sidewalk,
and the tuberose poodle together. Aging
men walk through the macadam auto ravines,
until magnolia dusk, and then they go to
their rooms, walking from faucet to window-hole.
They crawl under a mealy blanket seeking that
primeval night that came before creation, and
fall at once into a water sleep, void of
vegetable, animal or root.

The highways have no ancestors;
the 19th century American was kinless
iron, and these men of the
20th are houseless specters because

4

they have never claimed the continent.
They have destroyed the old, rooty
deities of the Cherokee and the Huron
which are now howling in their dead,
double-breasted coats and pants. The
city auto man has killed everything,
going through the unowned land without
branch, leaf, trunk or earth. The
autumn comes, and he has no foliage
to shed, and the winter appears, and
he cannot rest or sleep or die until
April, and his destiny star, too, is
dead. He has no green May shoots and
no loam in which to sprout. He feeds
listlessly and is alone when he genders
with his wife. He is an unseeding,
hating man who has forgotten to plant
a street, a blue-bell, a house.

Prophecy, O lost people without
a fate, is seeing the quick of the
instant. You have no porch, no yard,
no steps, you are groundless, and bitten
by gnats because you have slain the
earth. Can you die? Death is sweet
and dear, for it is quiet. But there
are no hills to appease you, and no
mountains to give you hard, striving
will, or rivers to wash your eyes to
make them see.

Homeless, denatured ghost of many
leafy races, where do you blow? who
will gather you up?

A DECLINE OF SOULS

"The statistician will register a growing progress, and the moralist a gradual decline: on the one hand, a progress of things; on the other, a decline of souls. The useful will take the place of the beautiful, industry of art, . . . and arithmetic of poetry. The spleen will become the malady of a levelling age."
Amiel

"I look on my generation with grief: its future is blank and grim: it will grow old in inaction, it will sink under the weight of doubt and barren science."
Lermontov

When Gogol had published *Dead Souls* one critic exclaimed he had never realized that Russia was such a tragic country. Gogol writes: "Let us admit, gentlemen, that life is very dreary." Are we no more than the deceased serfs in Gogol's novel or have we fallen into a long, political sleep? When we awaken from this lethargy, the result of Baal, the idol of comfort, what will the American Caliban do? De Tocqueville had predicted that the two great energies in the world would be the United States and Russia. Three decades ago at least forty million peasants left the farms to go into the factories of Leningrad and Moscow. A great many sinewy boys from the Midwest and South quit their bucolic hamlets and sold their mares to become hapless auto drudges in Detroit, Chicago and Pittsburgh.

Who could imagine that a Tartar's Utopia would be little else than a Byzantine Ford Motor Works, and that so much blood would be spilled to make people utterly wretched. One of the goriest jests was hatched by turning Russia into an alms-house governed by the Communist knout. Even Alexander Herzen, a remarkable thinker, could not have imagined what has occurred in the Soviet Union. He wrote: "Russia will never stage a revolution with the sole aim of ridding herself of Tsar Nicholas only to replace him by a multitude of other Tsars — Tsar-deputies, Tsar-tribunals, Tsar-policemen, Tsar-laws." But the feudal factory system obtains in the two corporate states. Cities have been turned into industrial battlefields, the tractor becomes a war tank, the farms abandoned, and communal and simple living has been cast off for solitude and expensive penury in crowded Moscow and New York. Montesquieu claimed: "The love of democracy is likewise that of frugality."

Spite of the Marxian shibboleths and the capitalistic flag of progress, the flesh of the workingman is the property of the government. The proletariat and the clerk are the victems of robber prices. The cost of products is changed every day; constant alteration in prices is guerrilla warfare against the people.

He is loot of the merchant, and besides does not even own his wages most of which are confiscated by the state and for his welfare! The plight of the impoverished inhabitants in America and the Soviet Union is miserable as that of the soldier and pleb during the age of Diocletian. At this time the pauperized Egyptian was less servile than the modern citizen. "The Egyptian is ashamed," says Ammianus, "if he cannot show his brown and lean body marked with welts upon welts received for refusal to pay his taxes."

What difference does it make whether the factory drudge is devoured by the cartels or the communist state. In either country he is duped by the puritan gospel of work. Not only his body but his privities are also chained; for it is considered libidinous to enjoy one's occupation. Compelled to be a feudal factory slave, making the same dull, repulsive rubber tires, auto parts, or shoveling gravel and cement, or piling store goods until the sun has disappeared, he is too tired to lie with his wife at night. Lumpish at the table he drearily swallows his packaged hamburgers and canned pears, and his head is as comatose as his pudendum. He is abstemious because he is prematurely impotent. His mind also slumbers and the worker who does not think or feel is Caliban who is snoring matter.

Rabble articles and the labor squandered in creating them hardens the heart. Nations that are rich in parasitic goods are poor in spirit. And his diction is no less somnolent and slothful. He chews the language, called jargon, with a jaded tooth. One who has little compassion for English abhors any show of emotion. The word, pity, has been expurgated from our national ethics. He lacks those virile sentiments which bind one person to another.

A pragmatical slave of the immoral corporation, he has adopted the cult of comfort. The eye of the farmer is as listless and septic as the mechanic's. Neither has the contemplative faculty; or the desire to sit on a shelving rock, regard the gray tuft of the sea, or consider Aristotle's remarks on neap tide. The upper classes are as thoughtless as the commoners; finally, we have achieved the classless society! For the rich and the poor hanker for the same whorehouse amusements and puerile gewgaws.

But there is one fiscal evangelism for the wealthy and another for the laboring masses. Nobody is so charitable as a dead millionaire or more parsimonious than a living one. Though he bequeaths his fortune to hospitals and churches after his death he goes about meek and ragged as a waif while he is alive. The American Plutus wears leather patches at his elbows or is photographed showing a hole in the sole of his shoes to indicate to the raving populace his indifference to expensive living. He is a clandestine hedonist who has taken the vow of poverty, for should an indigent friend require alms of him he is always out of pocket. But the credo of the poor is waste; he buys refrigerators, washing-machines, any brand new gewgaw in the market, which accounts for the immense resources of the body politic. Each man is, in great part, what he does and eats; what ails the laborer most is not his wages, but satiety. The mechanized multitude is plagued by a scorifying boredom, the machine and a police regimen. The hands and the legs of the American are paralyzed. He is prey to sundry diseases since he does not walk, and he is graved in a narrow, casket-shaped apartment in the vast garbaged cities or in the Sunday gas station towns.

The hands of the nation have died; so unaccustomed to use them he fails to shake hands with an acquaintance; besides, he has fallen under the spell of the coldest of goddesses, Hygeia. Afraid of touching anybody lest he be infected by a germ, he is unable to catch the most important of all human diseases, affection. For the like cause often he will not drink from his wife's glass, and in spite of his soporific lewdness, he considers copulation as no different from his evacuations.

The handless man is incapable of loving and so we have no amorous poems. There are no potters, kilns, cabinet-makers or tinsmiths. There were fourteen pewterers in the colonial Danforth household; Paul Revere's ride that was never finished is celebrated in our junkshops of education, but there is no mention of him as a silversmith who wrought lovely bowls and chalices. We reason from our hands to head, said Thoreau.

The factory grub wanders from one place to another, for this is the kinless age of Cain. His mind is *bokeless*, and kindness, the father of sociable feelings, is almost extinct in his breast. "We are not born for ourselves alone," said Cicero. He toils until the Wall Street speculator, and the banker, a euphemism for usurer, require an artificial panic. Deprived of his mortgaged home, the automobile he bought on credit as well as the marriage-bed he did not know depended upon permanent employment, he ranges a continent of hopeless, zero cities. His will has flagged; for the volition of the people is enervated by a plethora of conveniences he imagined he had purchased. Suetonius, referring to the avarice of Caligula, writes, "and divers times he brought a dearth and famine among the people by shutting up the garners and storehouses from the pleb." We are too complicated and devious to understand the humble economy of the Indian; when a Massachusetts lawyer refused to buy a basket he had woven, the red man said: "What, do you mean to starve me!"

Who inherits the spoils of the stricken workmen? The wastrel and the sharper. Solon demanded that each Athenian should reveal how he got his livelihood. An emperor of the Tangs held it as a maxim that if there was a man who did not work, or a woman that did nothing, somebody must suffer cold or hunger in the empire.

The national adoration of lucre is crueler than the veneration of the gory gods in the Aztecan oratories. The Spartans used iron coins so that if any unruly citizen had accumulated enough of this dross to fill a wagon he was still a man of humble means. Sir Thomas More divulged his hatred of riches by alleging that the toilet seats were made of gold. Recently the fiscal illuminati of one of the eastern universities decided that $100,000 should be spent in order to discover why lavatories are constructed with less engineering intellect than a missile. Nowadays what is important is where men excrete and not how they think. The American has relinquished the conceptions of the physiocrats for a watercloset! Alas, the cloaca has taken the place of sane customs and the adages of the sages, and this is progress.

The uneducated scientists and the deacon of Mammon have spoiled the vines, the comestibles and the American earth. Were it possible to know why man lives only to die, or even for what purpose he ever exists, one could comprehend human cupidity.

The people are ravaged by brand new baubles and mechanical conveniences that are not essential to their few contemplative lives.

Had one Job's balance who could weigh the guilt of the inventor, the scientific engineer, or the industrialist, who is the professor of greed.

This pawnbroker in Christendom lends money to the guileless populace so that they can fill their mortgaged homes with washing-machines, refrigerators, puce-colored bath tubs and fusty commodities at an interest no Shylock could ever have conceived possible. Who can count his wiles? His grossest hoax is the political one; he selects the millionaire masters of the people who suppose they will be their servants.

He sets up institutions and titles them trust companies. What a perfidious appellation and bestial oxymoron is trust company! Then he falsely advertises his consumers' goods, but who is consumed? The patrician money-lender records his lawless profits, canonized by the state and the church, in a doomsday ledgerbook the masses are incapable of interpreting.

Economic famines are almost as regular as the summer

solstices; during these seasons when there is no pasturage, and work for the laborer is withered, the country is a creditor's necropolis of automobiles, household furniture and foreclosed houses. The commoners, uninitiated in the orphic mysteries of finances, do not realize that the purchasers are always the borrowers and the hostages of the bailiff. "Cunning," said Hegel, "is the irony of brute force."

The legal thieves marry chorus girls, mechanized clothes-dummies referred to as models and illiterate stage buffoons, and their issue is the tow-headed dotard and the baby doll with the graveled voice.

The poor, white and black, are the illegitimate children who have been mocked and gulled by three words, morality, justic and principles, the father, the son and the holy ghost of usury.

Avarice is an impious enigma. Who requires a 1000 acres for his gullet and stomach? What can one family do with seven lagoons, several hotels, a cleuch, and eight homes? Those who acquire money for no other reason than to get more of it should be put in a madhouse. An excess of property or articles is unlawful as hunger. There is an ancient Chinese proverb: "If you have two loaves of bread, sell one, and buy a lily," which is a very artistic way of living. The compassionate man would give one of them to him who has not a crust.

There is another social plague, change. The consequence of constant alterations in fashion is a polity of freaks. The sidewalk is one of the few recreations of the multitude. Most of the fugitive rapture occurs in the street which resembles the public stews and a bedlam for nihilists. The luxury of a deluxe privacy is for the monied classes. But the average pariah is lucky to occupy an unpainted, fetid room two headstones in width and four long. In Ecclesiasticus it is told that man requires water, bread, clothing and a house to cover his shame.

The suits worn in Bohemia represent defiance and revolt. Women's hats look like the head of an ostrich or a chamber-pot. A female garbed in the trousers of Hercules the foot-soldier confuses the pudendum. When not hoveled in lesbic pants she goes abroad in a skirt that divulges her pillared loins. Outré garments are the pastime of a lubricous and thwarted public. The male burns for this depraved Messalina who is too costly and frigid an article; moreover, he cowers before the iron-boweled bitch. Beside himself, and undone, he becomes an onanist or turns to men. For the social reformer, with anile, political testicles, has banished the bawdy house and the government has endeavored to police the privities of the commonweal.

Utterly separated from the dollar social body, what remains to him but the surrealistic trance? Despising the Lilliputian aspirations of the everyday Plutus in tweeds, he joins the clandestine tribe of castaways who are poets, students and homosexuals.

Living alone, No-Thing is his nihilistic deity; his unpeopled emotions are hymns of narcotic suffering. Small wonder that Hart Crane, the gifted pathic, selected the following quotation out of the Book of Job as a superscription for *The Bridge:* "from going to and fro in the earth, and from walking up and down in it." Lucifer, the fallen star, hears only the steel harp strings of a bridge in his seamless, tumored sleep.

The carnal, pensive mammal is almost extinct as the mastodon painted on the massy boulders in Kansas. Where is a human being? is the cry from the ribs of the ambulatory skeleton on the pavements of the American megalopolis. Man has sunk into the ice and snows of his own solitude.

He is the expression of the cold products he makes: feeble, lustless goods — nylon, dacron and cellophane are the substitutes of wool, cotton and papyrus gathered from the warm, blooded lamb, picked in the living, seeded fields, mashed out of the bark of the wombed fig-tree.

The frigid store face is as empty of curd, butter and manual feeling as American bread. The hand and the foot have been devoured by the machine. Man is the four-wheeled auto sloth that vomits stygian gasoline fumes and smog as his belly slops along the asphalt.

Men in their beginnings are energetic, according to Thucydides. The health of the republic is the affection of the people for one another. The maker desires to associate with others; he craves a close kinship with the ground and his tools. "Thou shalt be in league with the stones of the field, and the beast in the field shall be at peace with thee."

Yesterday, which is 50,000 years, is a temporal sigh. The annals of Rome and the United States are indivisible. Pliny the Elder, despising the pravity of his country-men, thought the primitive Chauci, who lived without fruits or cattle, eating fish and goat's milk, were more civilized than the Romans. Man always looks backward for his arcadian ideals and imagines no better contentment than Shem in his tents. Any century appears better than our own. Should we have broken the Pillars of Hercules and passed over the Sea of Darkness? A sixteenth-century explorer called the New World *tierra damnata*. The colonists left England to settle a wilderness. By the time of Hamlin Garland the farmer was half-insane. This author tells how a family traveling in a covered wagon stopped to ask a stranger where was the road to the Dakota Hills. The itinerant wanderers were offered agricultural implements, a cow or two, fodder and help to revivify a neglected fallow would they remain and be his neighbor.

14

When the pilgrims were hacking the briars to found Concord they wept because although they were together each one was alone.

The American has never had the genius for attachment. Bacon was of the mind that those who lacked friends "to open themselves unto are Cannibals of their own hearts." Hawthorne was crestfallen because of his inability to love others, and Emily Dickinson, the New England sibyl, de-declared: "How good to be safe in tombs."

Our history is the tragedy of separation. The pioneer slew valleys and meadows that are more of a retribution than the forest of Nodh had been to Cain. He poured out the entrails of *tierra nueva*, poured slag and clinkers upon the rivers, built soulless, garage apartments and highways that are tunnels in Hades. The modern American city is an industrial battle-field, and the avenues thereof are macadam guts with fatherless names, A, B, and C.

Manhattan is an isle, but few indeed have any need of the mariner's eye. Where is the familial porch and the bucolic wooden gate-posts upon which Roman youths could smear marjoram to announce their troth?

Did we destroy the New England keeping-room, as sacred to the American householder as the utensils set aside for the idols of Latium, for the functional kitchen in a mechanic's society? Or did we dismember the bundling-room reserved for courtship to send boys and girls into alleys, robber streets and into the cinemas, our amorous vomitories, for their epithalamiums?

We have created what Amiel called "the epoch of the anthill."

Words to the human race, such as tillage, furrow, turf and sod have well-nigh vanished from the American vocabulary. How many professors, aliens in their own land,

15

know what are the tares, the chaff and the small cummin seed in the New Testament. In the *Haiku* it is written: "learning is as ordinary as eating rice at home." But education today has nothing to do with wisdom. The pedant is locked up in an academic cold storage for fools. After he has received his drossy Ph.D. he is appointed the shepherd of the college sheep. Our academies of Philistia are, as Lucian held, splendid statues of Jove or Neptune, made by Praxiteles, magnificent outside, but inside, the homes of mice and spiders.

"A great city is . . . a great solitude," said Aristotle, and so is a small town. Observe the funerary rites of a marred, touchless shopper in a self-service market: each customer is a sepulchral orphan; he walks and talks to himself. When he approaches the cashier and gives her the money for what he has bought she drops the change into the palm of his exiled hand without grazing the skin. This is supposed to be market-place sanitation. But people must exchange each other's germs or expire of the worms of Herod.

Auto and self-service are the new names for Narcissus who cares only for himself.

May no one assume that these granitic negations comfort me. I assert plainly as I know how that these words fall out of my troubled and roofless soul, and, as Jean Jacques Rousseau said: "Instead of ink I write with the water of Phlegethon."

KANSAS CITY REVISITED

A novelist is always writing the same book; for he is born to make the perfect poem or novel. That is why he keeps on writing books. The writer belongs to a tribe of men that remembers best, and yet he is always recollecting the same place, or city or childhood, and piecing together a particular river, maple leaf, sand bar, porch, the heady fragrance of a vacant lot sunflower, and when he is describing a room in one town, he is thinking about the depot dust or an orange he knew or nosed in his childhood. Sherwood Anderson wrote of the harnessmakers, and the smalltown hindrances and pronging oak trees of Winesburg Ohio, in a Chicago slummy furnished room. I have never forgotten how I imagined an Eighth Street Kansas City brothel smelled. The prostitutes occupied rooms upstairs over Basket's Chili Con Carne lunch counter, which was next to a saloon and the first lady barber shop in K.C., where part-time street-walkers and fast chippies cut the hair of round-shouldered ranchers from Lincoln, Nebraska, or Dallas, Texas. The woman who ran the place advertised her rooms for light housekeeping, which attracted brakemen, working on the M.K.T., or johnnies that repaired locomotives in the roundhouses. These decayed stores, located underneath the Eighth Street viaduct which rambled through Delaware and Baltimore Streets to the shambly depot, gave off a heavy odor of sin that sharpened the nostrils, and which was mingled with barber shop witch hazel, hair tonics and April Bock beer. When I was seven or eight I used to sit on the front doorsteps, and bored old codgers and railroad switchmen would

17

stop to give me a nickel or dime on their way up to inquire about light housekeeping. Ever since then vice has had that odor of those rooms, and so have Shakespeare's shames in the Sonnets.

To remember is the trade of the poet, but the greatest enemy of Mnemosyne is nostalgia, which is the stumbling block to perception. Everybody has the homesickness for the roots of place, and this malady is strongly revealed in contemporary fiction. One would then think that every one who has the nostalgia illness is an artist because he is the bondservant of place, which we have been embalming and sanctifying in the American Novel since Mark Twain's *Huckleberry Finn*. This is not the truth, and Twain, who pined for the Mississippi, and all those wretched mud-settlements and tatterdemalion steamboat towns that so often rotted in the great river floods, never had enough intellect or will to see these frontier, desperado towns as they were. *Roughing It* and *Tom Sawyer* are books of the Gilded Age and not the novels of wisdom. Twain scribbled humor books to laugh them off — those infernal wild west dance-halls, gullies, and ramshackles. Twain's humor was an uneasy evasion; when Twain had a rodeo bandit ride into a saloon town to shoot it up, he just guffawed. Twain and Dreiser were pessimistic, but both were doting mad for their memories. That is the real trouble with our fiction; it is talented, but puerile, and plain and simple homesickness. A great book is a double one; when Don Quixote is weary of the cudgels and the thrashings he gets from muleteers and tavern-catiffs, and is ready to simper at his own truths, Sancho Panza becomes his will, and tells his Master, Don Quixote, who is then the expiring and will-less artist, that he will go out under the stars to seek the Lady Dulcinea del Toboso. The poet's faculty is divided; it is Janus-faced, one cheek is at war with the past, but in the other is the dove and the olive branch which means that he is at peace with his memories. No poet can reflect a past with which he is not sorely at war; otherwise he ceases to be truthful and his chant is the siren's song which deceives the people. People love to hear Homer sing of Ithaca, of Abydos, of Agamemnon's land and of sandy Pylos where Nestor ruled; often the reader or the audience hearing the honeyed ballad of locality forgets the wrath of Homer. Despite all the pæans about a rugged Ithaca, we must not forget that when Ulysses returns no one recognizes him but his nurse. Penelope has been painted as the faithful, linen-spinning wife, but she is very wily, and entices the suitors she appears to be driving away. Many Greek poets coming after Homer said that she was by no means chaste.

Homer detested Ithaca, and let me admit, I hate Kansas City, which is still a wild, rough outpost town of wheat, railroads, packing houses, and rugged West Bottom factories. It is the burial ground of my poor mother, whose blood, like Abel's, cries out to me from every cobblestone, building, flat, and street of Kansas City. My mother and I came to Kansas City in 1906, from Dallas; she was a hard-working, buxom little woman, with a fragrant red calf's tongue she stuck out of her mouth when she laughed. We occupied rooms on McGee Street right off Admiral Blvd., and though we were very poor she had a great laugh in her small brown eyes, as wrinkled and sweaty as two salty olives. She laughed and joshed because she wanted to forget our poverty and also to strive against melancholia. McGee was in a rotten part of the city, but it was not evil in aspect; the houses were built of rock, set on hilly cobblestones, which were mapled and aldered, and there were plenty of porches overgrown with high speared grass and mustard-stinging

19

sunflowers. Dilapidated McGee was in the graveyard portion of the city, and still is, but the latticed porches with the grass tangled around them were very pleasant on Indian summer nights, and men sat outdoors in their B. V. D.'s, eating a half-pint of ice cream that cost five cents. People had tree and flower feelings about their streets, as you can see from the names, Cherry, Locust, Maple, Oak, Walnut, and all these tree streets belonged to the poor, or at least were occupied by them. Kansas City was still an agrarian town which had little of the abstract and theoretical coldness that modern city-makers have who take the appellations of their avenues from letters of the alphabet. McGee runs into Admiral Boulevard, below which were the rockribbed courthouse with Rhenish turrets and the livery stables. It was a great mule and horse market, and it was real pastime to go to an auction and watch Max Stedna, who ran the Fifth Street Stables, get rid of a senile nag he had doctored with arsenic. A lot of horsedealers came down for the show, and when a greenhorn bought a horse for his vegetable and watermelon wagon from Stedna, they blew their noses into bandana handkerchiefs and guffawed until they rolled in the dirt. On the other side of McGee is Eighth which is intersected by foliaged streets that run out to the Paseo, which was once high-tone and had a fine park cannon and a stone piazza that seemed to have been carved and dented by long rains and hotspring nymphs. It's a dingy colored section now, and though it is rough and has some of the wild and dirty lunacy of big-city poverty, grass and dandelions save it a little.

Walnut Street was my playground, and it was there that I saw Teddy Roosevelt in a parade showing the golden tooth smile of the Gilded Age. Politically, Roosevelt was a K.C. man, and the Kansas City *Star* was his paper. It was the culture sheet of the midwest. I remember two dissimilar events which were written up in the *Star* and of equal worth to me. In 1910 the *Star* had a long account of a famous count with a potato nose and a stringy Mongol beard who had died. There were many photographs of him; the beard made a considerable impression upon me, for I thought that the only men who wore beards were God and Robert Browning. I recalled the man's name for quite other reasons. He was Leo Tolstoy, and though he looked like an apostle he had the underlip of some carnal and fierce animal. At about the same time the *Star* gave two whole pages to Mr. Hagen who had just been shot by a jealous motorman. Hagen was a big Democrat whom my mother knew, and the motorman killed him for going out on long buggy rides with his wife. The *Star* showed the bullet holes in the buggy which Hagen, a man of large and fat affections, was driving on a country road beyond the city limits. He was a crony of Cromwell who had a commission house on lower Walnut. Hagen used to come and see Birdie, a skinny woman with refined glasses, who rented a room from my mother at 710 A East Eighth. Hagen and Cromwell were Jonathan and David to each other, and when Hagen was killed, Cromwell, a fine and dandy man, who never bothered with women, wept like a baby, as my mother said. Hagen, a masher and rounder, was deeply religious, and he died saying "Jesus is Mine." Cromwell, who used to sign notes when my mother needed a mortgage or a loan, never got over the death of Hagen, and neither did I. I remember his obesely trousered legs, and his Elk's Club throat when he sang to Birdie. There was something else about Alderman Hagen that remained with me. I used to brood about him, and began to think of Hagen and Leo Tolstoy together. Had Hagen taken the motorman's warning and stayed away from his wife, and hadn't been

21

Pierce Library
Eastern Oregon University
1410 L Avenue
La Grande, OR 97850

killed, Leo Tolstoy's picture would never have appeared in
the *Star* either, because the paper wouldn't have bothered
about him if he had not died. The two men became so confused in my mind that I later thought that Count Leo Tolstoy had been shot by the motorman while he was driving
his illicit sweetheart to Seltzer Springs in a horse and buggy.
Maybe I was not too far wrong, for Count Leo Tolstoy was
a rounder too, and ran mad for women as it is said in the
Book of Esdras.

My neighborhood was, and still is, the old sin town. On
the corner of Walnut my mother used to go to what she
called the dago fruitstand. The two boys I played with and
who never tormented or hurt me were the sons of the
fruitdealer. We went to George Washington Public School
on Independence Avenue, and every one, including Phineas
Levy, whose father was a Walnut Street jeweler, was afraid
of the Italian blackhands. But I never knew more gentle and
clean-looking boys than these two American-Italians who
robbed a mail train a few years ago! Fortunately, their father
had become a political boss, and everybody in K.C. who
knew these refined and docile boys were happy that they
were not sent to prison for robbing the government which
robs the people. That is at least the way a Kansas Cityan
had put it. Missouri is not the home of Jesse James and
Pendergast without reason; and the midwesterners, who
have a good, ripe hatred for federalism, have never been
able to see what law has to do with morals.

Below Walnut is Main, where the barber colleges used to
be, and then Deleware, where Schier had a wholesale liquor
business but made his money out of Tanlac, which people
took as a tonic during prohibition. The next street after that
is Wyandotte or Baltimore where the Baltimore Hotel stands.
Nat Goodwin, the comedian who had nine wives, stayed

there. The Baltimore is close to the classy K.C. Doric Temple, the Willis Woods Theater, where I saw Anna Held, and toward Twelfth are the broken-down movie lust houses. On Twelfth is the famous Muehlebach Hotel where Theodore Dreiser had Clyde Griffith in *An American Tragedy* work as a bellhop.

Kansas City is a smutty and religious town, and it did not take long for Dreiser's Clyde Griffith, who peddled salvation with his mission-house father, and sang hymns in the gutters, to go to the high-tone erotica palace, the Muehlebach. When I was last in Kansas City I met a goodlooking woman on the Troost Avenue street-car, and when she suggested that I meet her in the evening on the mezzanine floor of the Muehlebach I was sure she was a venereal queen.

People in Kansas City are wild about Christian Science, vice and lots of penance. There was Emma Moneysmith, the Mormon lady barber from Salt Lake City; she was addicted to Brigham Young and crazy for men. Not avaricious, she often fell in love with curly-haired boys from Wichita, or Armourdale, who were broke. But she had a son, Gerald, a fine Bible and fiddle boy, who looked like Buster Brown or a matinee idol, and she worried a great deal about his education. Gerald's father was a Salt Lake Mormon and had gone his own polygamous way, and Emma had brought him up as an orphan; so that whenever Emma met a man she did not love, but who had money, she thought of Gerald's education, and skipped town with his purse. One day poor Emma was also shot in the Kansas City *Star*; there was a whole front page about her and a Greening, Wyoming cowboy whom she had jilted, after taking his savings account, telling him that it was better to take his money than to be unfaithful to him. My mother cried over Emma, and said that she was a fine straight little lady who was only watching out for Gerald's future. Years later, Gerald, who had become a fine violinist in an Omaha movie theater, came to see my mother, and they both wept all afternoon over Emma.

There was Mrs. Harney who had a lot of Christian Science emotion and a bad appendix. She was rawboned and large and amorous, and kept some gold teeth in her mouth to attract men, and dyed her old-looking hair a spoiled carrot red for the sake of appearance. Her great fancy was Gilman, a Rogers silverware salesman from Cleveland. After Gilman left she took up with Drew who had small, pink hands which he often lathered. Harney liked a man that smelled of soap. Her friend was strict Catholic Mary who had a room in my mother's Eighth Street flat. Catholic Mary never looked at a man and wore high boots to shield her ankles. She said that if women covered themselves men would keep their minds on church and business. Mary hated lewd beer bottles and cans and spent her evenings sewing and in Bible thoughts. One evening the viaduct saloon-keeper came to the flat to tell my mother to invest in Tulsa oil, and passing by Mary's door which she always kept open so that nobody could ever accuse her of entertaining a man, saw her booted foot and reeled. He pleaded with my mother for an introduction, although she told him she was a man-hater and would never look at a common saloonkeeper. But he bought her cutglass and a ruby ring and soon they ran off to Omaha where they lived with unusual, illegal happiness. Vice ought to be a little concealed; today men look with the most feeble eyes at a woman's breast, or at the subtlest points of her nipples, but they would marry a woman at once if she knew enough to hide herself more.

Neither my mother nor I ever got out of these low, wicked streets. She played the piano to keep herself refined and kept old, faded postcards of bygone or dead friends or Swope Park views which she contemplated when she was sad and urgently wanted lofty reveries. On Sundays we took streetcar rides to Swope Park for air and elevated thoughts, and it was a fine tonic to pass the exchequer green lawns, and the monied rock houses in Country Club or in the swell Rockhill residential sections. My mother had considerable animal wisdom about human beings, but she was a midwestern wildcatter when it came to money. She invested her savings in wells that never gushed, and once put about eight hundred dollars into a new imitation rubber. She was quite dreamy about synthetic hot water bags, sanitary cups, and antidisease ice cream soda glasses and straws. Frontier Baptist and Mary Baker Eddy towns have always been frantic about sanitation. These cities, which are full of every kind of man and woman dirt, and have the most repulsive sex and movie dives, and prurient penny arcade nudes, and pornographic post card streets like Twelfth, have citizens, who are crazy about the word CLEAN. Clean health, clean living, clean politics! Only the corrupt can use this tabu word so easily.

I tried very hard to get my mother to buy a little property as a real estate investment out near Fifteenth Street where the new Coca-Cola skyscraper had been erected, and several blocks from where the railroads were going to put up a 50 million dollar union station. She was afraid of speculation, she said, although any stranger could talk her into investing in Kansas gas wells, or a share in a horse race track. She was a gambler, and got very scared when she was offered something safe, and often told the person that she was from Missouri and nobody could take her for a fool. Poor mother, she was from Missouri all right! My mother also wanted to become an optometrist. A transient roomer, a

25

regular fellow from Denver, carried a sample case of lenses. He said he could teach my mother to be an optometrist in a few weeks, and that they could open up a fine eyeglass store in Denver. My mother found out he had a wife and children, and besides she had been in Denver years before, and said Pike's Peak did not agree with her, and that the consumptives just dropped on the sidewalk every day.

I wish my mother had bought land in the Rockhill district where the University of Kansas City now stands. She was a right moral little lady who never deceived anybody which is why she was such a dupe herself.

Nobody ought to return to his native city; it's a premature burial, and yields nothing but a terrible sickness of the mind. I went back to memorize Cherry and Locust and Maple Streets, and to take a look at a gaunt miserable shop at 16 East Eighth Street underneath the viaduct.

Ay, go to your native city, but why? It is buried deep down in the loamy cairn of identity in which one can plant everything without going anywhere. Socrates said it was foolish to travel since one always took oneself along anyway. He also said that one mountain, one vale, and one sea divulges everything. One Kansas City, my Mother City, her Tomb, for all her defeats are interred there, and my own; we mourn for our memories and hate them. I need never go back, for my mother lies in the hurt and open sepulchre of my soul, and another return to her could only be a rough and barren pain that I do not require either for a book, or for my life, or for my Mother.

TEARS OF THE VIRGIN

Is Spain still the flower known as *Lágrimas de la Virgen,* Tears of the Virgin? The late Miguel de Unamuno and Pío Baroja had fallen into a great despondency over the corruption and Europeanization of their country. Both decided to walk through the Iberian Peninsula and talk to the peasants to see whether they had escaped the depravity of modern civilization. It is a very fatiguing journey by train, for most of the earth is mountainous, and as wondrously sterile as the salt marshes in Cadiz, the ancient city of Hercules; but these two old savants went on foot from one pueblo to another. They returned believing there were peasants dwelling in the earthenware hill towns, alongside dry river gorges, and in the midst of the olive yards, who had not succumbed to the infamy of money or foolish ambitions.

Strabo, the ancient geographer, said the Spaniards were crafty and thievish, and Seneca, according to Tacitus, born in the old Moorish and Jewish town of Cordoba, was a usurer. Spite of their toothless *peseta* smiles they may be less hardened by modern life than occidental people. It is common enough to see a father sitting on the threshold or on the step in his doorway on soft Mallorquin evenings repeatedly kissing and fondling his child. The humblest *obrero* has that breeding of the heart we look for in a poet or thinker. A seamstress or housewife seldom fails to greet the passer-by with a *"buenos tardes."* Upper class virgins or matrons do not speak to men in the *calles,* and are almost as closely guarded as they were in the time of Cervantes.

A family man is generally quiet and courteous, but the

youth, as everywhere else today, are insolent and rough with women, which is a Levantine custom. In old Athens Solon had to import whores to protect the Hellenic maids. The *criadas*, porters, or muleteers are far less diffident in their relations and amours. Though the houses of ill-fame have been shut, prostitution is rife. A former zipper-salesman from Brooklyn, who came to Mallorca to be a painter at the age of fifty, hired a pretty *criada* who later decided to become a street-walker because she wanted to earn more money. In southern Spain, and in Sevilla, a maid servant gets about two hundred and fifty *pesetas* a month, a little over five dollars.

Each Spanish province seems to produce special traits; mountainous people are rude, obstinate and as proud as the Solymi in the *Odyssey*. The Andalusian is dour, and the stubborn Basques in the Pyrenees can be recognized, as Anthony Kerrigan writes in his remarkable English translations of those two Basques, Unamuno and Pio Baroja, by their triangular faces. An Euclidean countenance is the best; Plato said that the pentagram was the symbol of goodness, and Pythagoras referred to people and thoughts as geometrical figures.

The Spaniard is a great idler. George Borrow, in *The Bible in Spain*, which was such a joy to Sherwood Anderson, said they ought to exert themselves more and call less on Jupiter. However, it is yet to be proved that being a drudge all day long in a factory or office is not abundant waste. The men sit at the cafes, or stand by the hour, while the women scrub their shirts and drawers on the rocks of the mountain streams. The male is an indifferent shopkeeper; though far from stupid, he becomes very confused when he has to give change; he cheats himself as often as he does his customer. Arithmetic is very bad for a nation, and is the source of avarice unless it has to do with navigation or the stars.

Civility is traditional; at Segovia, a comfortable city for epicures, situated on a plateau, eighty meters below which are peacocks screaming in the tree branches, is a cafe, Meson de Candido. It sits almost beneath the ancient Roman aqueduct, and the walls of this hostelry are decorated with photographs, not of street-gamin actors or ignorant athletes, but of Ortega y Gasset, Jimenez, Unamuno and Pio Baroja. When I asked the patroness of the inn for a glass of water, she said, giving me a carafe of wine, "Water is not good enough for an author." A man of letters in Spain is a Don and not the castaway Ishmael of America. When an article on me appeared in the *Baleares* in Palma, the man who sold ice in a two-wheeled cart drawn by a burro embraced me.

Is this Elysium? Alas, only Menelaus and the dead go to such fields of peace and flowers. There is much poverty here; one imagines that Spain is very dirty. Catullus wrote that the primitive Spaniards scrubbed their teeth with human urine; the *Zuñis* who lived in the legendary seven cities of Cíbola used the same excretions to moisten their adobe bricks, and the cleanly Danes at Bornholm, an island in the Baltic, mix cow dung with their paints.

The *moscas,* flies, are infernal pests in the south; at Torremolinas at a pension, I held a fly swatter in one hand, and rather furtively put food into my mouth with the other to outwit these peevish insects. The bread is seldom covered, and though it is charming to see a maid-servant carrying long unwrapped loaves under her maroon Arabic arm as she walks in the dusk between the plane trees, it hurts the imagination at table.

But despite the poverty, the Mallorquin women, whose ancestors are Phoenician, Greek, Roman, Berber and Jew, wear their hair carefully plaited, and their skirts and starched petticoats are as crisp and multicolored as phlox.

Spain is as filthy and as clean as any other land. The streets are not littered with trash or empty tin cans, fortunately too expensive for the Spainard. The rivers, which flow through rocky gorges in winter, are dried up in July and August, and would be a vast delight to the eye were they not offensive to the nose.

A Spanish pueblo has cobbled or dirt roads, and in front of the houses are pots of hydrangeas and begonias. At Santa Maria, fifteen kilometers or so from Palma, the walls of the homes are covered in the Fall with red pimientos. Even Inca, the shoe-town, has little, tidy cafes and the citrus and almond orchards which placated the indignation of the prophet Isaiah.

The *calles* of industrial Madrid and Barcelona are dispiriting as the wicked slums all over the world. The mire in the native quarters of a rustic village, and the sows rooting there, are far preferable to the diseased cement gut of the occident. There are far more cockroaches in a monied, affected Park Avenue apartment than in the neat rooms of an impecunious Spaniard. The poorest native, unless he is a beggar, and there are many, has at the rear of his dwelling or flat a patio covered with lemon and fig-trees, oleanders, and myriads of geraniums, zinnias, marigolds, and jasmine bushes. One can sing of penury, if it is not desperate, with far greater skill than of riches. "God bless indigence," said the late Eric Gill, for it is surfeit that kills the letter and the spirit.

Most of the mainland resembles the olive yards of ancient Israel, and this is the work of male hands, though women, too, labor in the fields. Between Gibraltar, a stupid English rock, and Cadiz, is a forest of cork trees which are bled by

30

stripping the bark. Cairns of neatly arranged wafers of cork, that look like St. John's bread, lie at the root of the blood-red trunks. As one goes into Sevilla there are leagues of olive groves set in the earth looking like red potter's clay upon which the porkers and brown goats graze, and at ancient Elche there is a forest of palm trees.

The Iberian coast is rather bare; in the south the blue and white villages prevail; they are lovely but mournful sepulchres, wondrous to contemplate, but not to inhabit. Mijas, a mountain hamlet, miraculously wrought by human hands, has the smallest bullring in Spain.

A great deal of the past has been eradicated in Andalusia; the hot winds from nearby Africa blow over the farms and the few ruined towers imagined to have been erected by Hercules and Odysseus. It is fabled that Menelaus also came to Phoenician Iberia. Marbella, along the coast, is about fifty kilometers from Malaga, where the widow of Goering and many rich Nazi officers now live.

Sevilla is a handsome dead city, the detritus of a great age. The gothic cathedral at Sevilla joins a Moorish court of orange trees which give off the voluptuous scent of a seraglio; in the sacristy of this church is a small painting of a crucified Christ with delicate, pained limbs. It is the only Murillo I have seen that is moving or even tolerable. Within one of the chapels is a dreary catafalque where the consecrated remains of Cristobal Colón are interred. The latter is as great a hero as Jason was in Hellas, and the modern Spaniard cannot understand why Americans celebrate the Admiral of the Seas as an Italian, when it was Isabella of Castile who gave him the money to fit out his caravels to sail beyond the Pillars. At Burgos I stayed in the venerable building, my window overlooking a patio with a lovely Nereid, a fountain of running water, where Ferdinand and

Isabella received Cristobal Colón after his second voyage.

Triana, the suburb of Sevilla, is the birthplace of the Emperor Trajan; it was formerly connected with Sevilla by a bridge of boats, and was a den of gypsies, thieves, and *mala gente*, bad people; it has since sunk into a dreary factory town where ordinary tiles and ceramics are made.

Aside from the cathedral, the alcazar, a palace of the Moorish kings, and the *Barrio de Santa Cruz*, which is the Jewish and Moorish quarter, Sevilla is not a city to awaken the intellect.

Malaga, where Picasso was born, and Valencia, are comfortable, boring cities, originally Arabic, and only resorts for the bourgeois merchants whose wives vie with one another in dressing their little girls in the most elaborate clothing. But Cordoba, the old capital of the Caliphs, is a town of many flowers and exquisite patios. The Mosque at Cordoba, a Moslem house of flesh, had a grove of 1200 crimson, marble pillars when it was built in the 8th century, and is carnal as Solomon's bedchamber.

Salamanca, conquered by Hannibal in 200 B.C., and perhaps ancient as Lisbon, supposed to have been founded by Ulysses, is more vigorous. The plaza of Salamanca is a visionary rectangle; it is surrounded by sandstone houses which shine at night like the gold of Ophir. On nearly every side of the piazza are cafes where Miguel de Unamuno, rector of Salamanca University, sat and argued. This last Aetna of Spanish philosophy vomited forth his fire until three or four o'clock in the morning. The owl of Minerva can be said to sit on the head of the Spaniard who does not eat dinner until eleven or midnight, after which he has his conversation. The city does not really awaken until evening vespers. Then the peripatetic Spaniard can be seen on the plaza of Salamanca, the Rambla in Barcelona, or the Borne in Palma. Throngs fill the cafes even on Sunday, the day of John Calvin and Stygian gloom in northern Europe. This holy day is far easier in Spain, for the streets are not a funerary, peopleless vault.

The buildings of Salamanca are Renaissance, though so much Spanish architecture is baroque, which is far less ornate than I had imagined. There is a virile, nude giant on the portal of the *Casa de Dos Aguas* at Valencia, resembling Nimrod the Hunter, or a titanic pederast from Gaza, which is done with vascular puissance.

In the rooms of Salamanca's medieval university, the Plateresque facade of which was added later, students pored over the works of St. Thomas Aquinas, Anselm, and Origen. To the secular professor the erudition of the schoolmen is passionate nonsense, but could it be drearier than the mediocrity of modern education? I am still of the mind that Loyola's conception of education as a discipline is correct. He asserted that "a pupil should be a corpse in the hands of a teacher." This is a mordant figure of speech, and paradoxical enough to express with startling energy the passive manner with which one should read a poem or listen to a sage. Today, the shallow prentice to knowledge puts on heavy armour as a protection against the influences of a good book or teacher so that he is absolutely immune to intellectual wounds.

Spain is the most Jewish of all the countries in Europe. When Cristobal Colón set out to cross the Sea of Darkness, he saw endless queues of Jews who were quitting the land rather than fall under the yoke of the Inquisitors, one of whom was a Jew. Many, however, remained in the country of the olive, fig, the palm and the almond trees of their new Jerusalem. Some feigned to accept Catholicism, but had an underground synagogue. Others were true proselytes.

Before the cruel ostracism Jews were ambassadors of the Pope; they were the most learned navigators of their times, and great travelers, as was Rabbi Benjamin de Tudela.

Antisemitism in Spain, as elsewhere, came from the early fathers of the primitive church, particularly Eusebius who poisoned eighteen hundred years by recording the apocryphal rubbish about the martyrdom of the Apostles. Though he admits that the first fifteen bishops of Jerusalem were Jews, he claims, without any historical evidence, that John and James the sons of Zebedee were decapitated by the Israelites, and that James the Just, brother or cousin of Jesus, met his visionary end at the hands of a Jewish laundryman who hit him on the head with a club.

The intellectual classes today are political dissidents and most of them are notoriously pro-Semitic. The late bishop of Sevilla, a Catholic bigot and overt friend of Israel, was a Jew. In front of Salamanca University is a modern statue of Fray Luis de Leon, the sixteenth-century Catholic poet, who was Jewish. The pathetic stall and window, where St. Teresa, the Jewess of Avila, confessed, is a most pious relic today.

There are no more than three synagogues left in Spain; the most poignant chamber of Elohim is in Toledo, near the house of El Greco, where are the master's paintings of the twelve Apostles, is done in Moorish style, but is not a room of pagan idols as are all the Christian basilicas glutted with Christs, Virgin Marys, and the crypts of dismembered saints.

Cordoba has one temple where Moses Maimonides, author of the renowned Talmudic commentaries, *The Guide for the Perplexed*, went to worship the God of Israel. It has no benches or chairs, containing only the holy cabinet for the ark. It is simple and small enough for all the piety that is left in man. This Arabic, abstract room of monotheism presses down upon the imagination until one sheds the driest tear, our historical remorse.

Although Christian worship is Hebrew and pagan, the Spanish Inquisitors regarded the cabbalists and Talmudic thinkers as sorcerers. Catholic priests were often suspected of being secret practitioners in the arts of Black Judaism. Many of the padres had come to view Christianity as the veneration of idols and the adoration of the Sainted Mary as theological venery. George Borrow wrote of an ecclesiastic, accused by the *Santa Casa* of Black Judaism; in his house beneath the floor was found a "wooden chest in which was a small shrine of silver, enclosing three books in black hog-skin" which were volumes of "Jewish devotion, written in Hebrew characters."

The church was the last great bastion of the communal artist. The art of the Catholic painter and sculptor was Semitic and heathen in conception. Those who sang in stone or in paint had sensibilities of Jeremiah or Hosea. There is scarce a church in Spain that is without a Hebrew prophet, Abraham, Noah, Moses, Jeremiah and Isaiah.

The Jews were remarkable artisans, and often their services were coveted by churchmen. There was a highly skilled Jew who carved wood, and the Spanish clerics at the Convento de Santo Tomas in Avila, who wanted him to make the choir-stalls, desired first to proselytize him. As they were unsuccessful they employed him anyway; for fifty years he labored, without violating the Mosaic tenets, for he made chairs for the devotees of Christ without a single figure or image, which is the beginning of idolatry and of painting. By the time he had completed his work he was an old man, and, too infirm to oppose the priests who had become his friends, he adopted their faith.

In Palma there is a street known as the Calle de la Plateria where Jewish silversmiths worked in former times, but which is now clogged with trashy shops for tourists, and watchmakers' stores. The shopkeepers, the debris of the quondam proud Sephardics, are Catholics with furtive faces.

The power of the church in Spain is enormous, but the attitude of the populace, even when devout, is ambiguous. There is too much poverty and there are too many priests, aged padres, with large Hittite noses, and faces worn out with prayer, who often sit in the shops of their relations. Many are worldly. It is bizarre to see a priest in a black cassock draped over a motorcycle speeding toward Gethsemane. One day I saw a nun on the Avenida Calvo Sotelo picking her nose, which may be pious; I don't know.

However, the Romanesque and Gothic churches of Spain are amazing and contain figures in every sinning posture; the capitals of the columns of the monastic court at Seo de Urgel are ornamented with griffins, lions, eagles and goats which are pagan symbols of Eros. The sandstone cathedral in Palma, which Havelock Ellis thought the finest in the world, though I don't know why, has a gargoyle, which is a man on his knees ready to vomit when it rains. The portals and friezes of the Spanish cathedral are pagan bestiaries; the satyrs, oxen and asses are stones that flow with spermaceti. Magog and Og, carved on the holy portals at Avila, are immense, hairy men as they are said to be in Genesis, which is a marvelous spectacle to the Spaniards, those short, obdurate stumps of Phoenicia.

The Gothic is sublime in agony, and no matter how hedonistic the art, Mary, mother of Jesus, whom William Carlos Williams refers to as the glorious whore, and Magdalene will always be virgins. Man was born to sin, and he cannot be obscene when he wonders about God, the Universe, and the sainted Marys whose skirts he kisses with such erotical piety.

36

The medieval church is a vast cranium of suffering stones, and the vault shows the agonized ribs of the body of Christ. Golgotha is the place of the skull. The reverence of stones is a primitive custom; Bethel, a pile of sacred rocks, is the hypaethral house of God which Jacob built. Kybele, the mother of the earth in Greece, was a black stone; Astarte was a fallen star or an aerolite. There is a statue of St. Jerome praying with a skull at his feet in Burgos; and at Valladolid, the same saint, carved by Alonso Berruguete, beats his chest with a rock.

There are many Berruguetes in the Colegio de San Gregorio in Valladolid which is a lazar-house of bloody Christs, wooden figures with the crucifixional nails and the blood painted on the hands and feet lying in glass caskets. This is repulsive but didactic art, the sacral lesson people are reluctant to accept — do not flee from the sorrows of others. It would be a mistake to assume that these halls of Golgotha are dedicated solely to misery and death; in the same Museum there is a carved figure of the thief whom Jesus said would go to Paradise; his hair flows down his back like Apollo's, and his naked hams are voluptuous as a woman's.

As long as the burro and the wagon do not disappear, hope cannot be abandoned. The peasant Mallorquin houses, made of unhewn stones, which have granite hearths and floors, kindle the most sluggish pulses. Western man has fallen into a long sleep; without legends, which are real history, he is dead rather than quick. Man goes to fables as he does to the incorporeal gudgeons and the barley loaves or starves his soul to death.

I know that a foreign land is as impermeable to me as the metaphysics of another person. If what I have written is solipsism rather than history, I hope the reader will pardon me, for I can do no better.

ROME AND AMERICA

Jacob Burckhardt's beautiful study of three hundred years of Roman history, veiled in moral ironies, should make the reader think a great deal about America. Our colonial lawgivers had the rude hardihood of a Romulus and Remus, and the early seventeenth-century New Englanders founded tree-shaded white frame villages as chaste as Alba, the white wooden village built by Aeneas and celebrated by Virgil. Rome had its fables, gods, bucolic commonwealth, and poetry, before it deteriorated and fell into the debaucheries of a Messalina. The lament of the poet, Propertius, who tells us about the rustic porkers that rooted in the dirt streets and on the hills of Rome, is about the same as Sherwood Anderson's verbal pining for the old Populist and handicraft Ohio towns.

The difference between the Roman and the American empire is that we are now adopting the licentious habits of a Poppaea, or a Commodus, or a Domitian, without having first acquired stable customs, deities, or a civilization. And we are about to become a soldier nation without any real knowledge of Europe, Asia, or the Orient.

The problem confronting Marcus Aurelius, Severus, Diocletian, was how to control the Prætorian guard who assassinated as well as appointed the rulers, most of whom were Thracian shepherds, stupid giants from Gaul, muleteers from the Danube provinces, fierce Goths from outpost regions. These street-gamin Caesars, very able soldiers, cruelly taxed the serfs and impoverished the urban plebs. The maladies of aging Rome were revolutions, crime, barrenness, and taxes. Prices had grown disreputable and burdensome, and speculation in foods so wanton, by the time of Diocletian, that that emperor felt he had to impose maximum costs on several hundreds of things, including grain, ordinary table food, livestock, clothes. Soldiers were robbed of their pay by a single purchase, and a peasant paid almost two and a half days' wages for a pair of shoes. Mutton and lamb were prohibitive, and Falernian wine, hymned by the Latin poets, was not for the lower classes who lived in the wealthiest city in the world.

Livy said that the downfall of Rome was brought about by insolence; rudeness was so great in his time that the lord of historians wrote that a blush was a mark of noble lineage. Gibbon wrote that the disintegration of the family household was the cause of Rome's decay. Emperors without offspring were a sign of a sterile populace. We know that the vilest boudoir acts of the feminine Caligula were imitated by the people. Anyone who reads St. Augustine's diatribes against the lascivious deities of the hinge and the door, or Lucian's mockery of homosexual Zeus, can see what was occurring in Rome.

Along with such turpitudes and broiling satiety came national apathy, that is, human indifference to the penury of others. Severus was the absolute sovereign of pitilessness. Little wonder that Caracalla, the son, was ruthless as his father, Severus, and that the living dregs of the Empire were no better. Caracalla had made so many attempts on the life of his father that Severus was said to have whispered to the young man, "Do not let them see you kill me." Does not this describe the full horror of unfilial, nihilistic Rome?

After Caracalla came the depraved Heliogabalus, who, Suetonius said, had not revealed his cormorant gut until he had ascended the throne. Heliogagalus surrounded himself with dancers, athletes, jugglers, barbers, and actors. It was Plato who warned the Athenians against the rule of actors and entertainers, which we in some real measure have in America today. The late Roosevelt often called varlets of the screen and stage to his table, which reminds us of Domitian, who gathered around him jugglers and dwarfs, and who relieved Roman economy by abating the price of the eunuch!

Diocletian's reign is a sort of historical curio. This emperor avoided Rome, repairing to a trans-Adriatic city, just as Hitler sought seclusion in an Alpine hamlet. Like Hitler he believed in omens and had many soothsayers around him. Like Caracalla, who built magnificent baths, now the litter of marble and stones in neglected vineyards and ravaged graveyards, he had almost as morbid a passion for building as the chancellor of a U.S.A. university. He modeled his reign upon that of the virtuous Marcus Aurelius but he taxed the people implacably. Peasants in his time, renting land, were mercilessly tithed for crops and huts. As Ratzel has written, "In the beginning was the ground-rent."

America has produced no annalist to be placed alongside Livy, Suetonius, Gibbon or Jacob Burckhardt. What is conspicuous in Parkman, Prescott, and the Spanish discoverer-chroniclers is not intellectual faculty, but energy. But the shape of our present is an invitation to a moralist on Burckhardt's model. It does not take much perception to see that we are on our way to the rigid social order of a Diocletian. And we may not have the luck to get a Christian renascence.

HOW DO YOU SPELL FOOL?

"I fear no mood stamp'd in a private brow,
When I am pleas'd t'unmask a public vice."
                                      Ben Jonson

A good writer is a gifted reader, and there is as much genius in Shakespeare's, Euripides' or Plutarch's reading as in their works. Every vision has been patched together from the works of notable sages, and most books are a cento. When writing flags it means that people are forgetting how to study, and no longer go to Seneca or to Cicero or to Blake to fortify their character. The poet must go to the hills, the valleys, the strong rivers of a fine versemaker to strengthen his nature. The greatest fault with my critic is that he is a weakling reader.

A man ought to have anise, garlic, savory bread and water-cresses in his writing, for that is good health to the mind, but this is a lunatic season for the writer. There is such a great dearth of integrity among authors that even an honest writer without talent is taken for genius. No wonder then that many are deceived by toadeaters who pretend that a pismire is a honeycomb, that a grasshopper mind is a seer, that a boy who wears the embroidered drawers of Paris is a girl and that a sick book is potent realism because it smells like a corrupt and dying animal. What is more important than being original, which has become the curse in poetry, is to learn what one is doing, and why one is doing it, and to say it without being perverse about it. See how many sophisms there are about writing. Some pretend that they

---

Reply to a review of *The Flea of Sodom.*

write to be alone, although they have already achieved the wildest solitude and still are museless. Others declare that they do not write to be read, and then lament the oblivion they have wooed. Such conditions make for the most froward minds, who see that we live in benumbing city desolation and call this progress, and who do not try to understand that the apotheosis of syntax and the invention of the printing-press have got nothing to do with human culture. Learning how to write has made people sly, and the printing-press is a malefic business monster, for few truthful verses are published, and though books are dispersed everywhere, a writer has to go to some slain street or garbaged building or to a crannied American town to find a fissured and lonley soul and more often than not he is likely to stumble into a poetaster.

It does not matter that he mislikes *The Flea of Sodom*, for as Robert Burton of the famous *Anatomy of Melancholy*, and whose greatest talent is in his erudition, says, "If you do not care for my book, go and read another." What troubles me is that he has so nimbly hid it. It appears that spleen and malice can do today what wise abilities cannot, for the reviewer jumps about the page like the Bible Nimrod who is said to have had a gnat in his head, and one has to look closely to find out why my book has brought up so much bile in him. People seldom look for symbols, but rather peruse a volume for easy swinepen shibboleths, and so we have today not human or symbolic scholars but political and social pedants.

When this scribbler calls me a fascist he means that I would rather eat olives, celery and citrous fruits and a barley bread with Aristophanes and Euripides than sit at table with Karl Marx, a good enough fellow in his own way. I am no working-class mystagogue who regards a riggish fruitdealer who sells carrots, peas and persimmons at four times their value as my benefactor, or the grubby grocer who changes his prices more often than Proteus his shape as my virtuous Cato. I do not care about the working-classes, the professional people, or the writing classes, but what is essential to me is honest workmanship, learning and human poetry. When costs are thievish, and that skulking Barabbas dough is called bread, insolence is everywhere, malice is swollen, amorous verse is dead and the state is despotic. There is a small sodality of puling minds for whom this point of view is more pernicious than beating one's father, lusting after a mother or lying with a uterine sister.

Tyranny is a pestilence and what I call the garage proletariat is most vulnerable to despotism because they have altogether surrendered to the flag of wages and are so slavish as not to know that more money does not mean more justice or better wisdom or more love. Wages alone do not make for human health. The hands have become crusty, stupid, and unlearned in affections. Factory workers are fragmentary persons and they handle nothing that is entire, and they have not their whole faculties for affection or friendship or for craftsmanship; rubber tires and automobiles are not signs of quiet and repose, but are more like spiders and tarantulas which, like a whore rather than a lover, are always stinging without bringing any contentment. Men are not so much oppressed by miserable pay as by the radio, the newspaper, and that jumping up and down invention, television; everything we do is for going somewhere else, and a people who have no strength to sit still and think are ready for any sort of change, upheaval or debacle. They cannot be quiet enough to read or love a wife. A great deal of sodomy is just a dithering male who is too nervous and too unsure of himself to take what is becoming the worst hazard today, entering a woman.

There has been much babbling about those who think with their blood, but a man ought to use whatever he has for his meditations. In some the hands are parables and in others the head is a mole creeping out of its hole with furtive meekness; and again it is the libidinous foot with which a man shows his art. Now which is more guileful, the mind or the blood, would be hard to say, for everything is so double at present that he whose words may rain as proudly as Zeus and who has a striding soldier front like Agamemnon, delicately jiggles his hunkers in the rear. Those that say they are rationalists and claim that they are guided by reason, scratch themselves the way Adam did, and when they hear Judith's sandals it is their itch that advises them. Bottom the weaver tells us that reason and feeling do not keep company nowadays, and though I respect mammoth heads like Aristotle, and marvel at the Euclidean intellect with which Marx squared and triangled money and labor, I trust Bottom.

But let us return to the quandary. Some persons derive more underground debauched pleasure in misreading Homer, or Euripides, or Plato than in comprehending them. A homeric line has so much primal strength that it would appear that the Smyrna bard used the Pelian ash of Achilles for a pen. Homer also has doughty ideas about food, and some may think that his plain table is for war and martial feeders, but I believe that he always has in mind what is best for a just commonwealth. He had scant regard for forced meats and dainties because he believed that they emasculate the will and pervert morals and intelligence. For example, forceless Menelaus has an Asiatic disposition and his palace has brazen floors and silver lintels, but Nestor, who is wise stable custom, sits on simple stones polished by the oil from the olive. Persons who mistake Homer for a

44

lover of Mars forget that he is writing of the ten years' Trojan war and not about Solomon's bedchamber. Heraclitus sharply rebukes Homer because he wanted to banish strife from the world. Shakespeare is read as perversely as Homer, and many do not realize what state-fear there was in him as his abhorrent, state-boweled Volumnia, mother of Coriolanus, shows. Theoreticians pore over the amorous plays with Ricardo or Adam Smith or Kropotkin in their minds, and this is foolish, for they forget that the Sonnets are the heart's Golgotha.

Do we know what we are seeing when we read "One law for the Lion and the Ox is Oppression," that fuddled ninnies mistake for an apothegm out of Zarathustra, described by them as a Junker state dithyramb, but which comes from Blake. The lion in Blake is not the ravening beast that it is in Dante's *Inferno*, but stands for moral vigor, and the ox for the bovine mind. First I fear most the brain without feeling, and after that the brave lion words about justice and goodness, and truth and poetry, when it comes from the mouth of the ox, or worse from dainty drawers, and I am not speaking of Bathsheba's underwear.

People that read without an abundance of emotion are as famished as they were before they opened its pages. We are hungered and thirsty, but how can we turn the gray water words in the earthen Cana books into wine without much loving. How easy it is to go to a great poet with a small listless heart, and with morose surd ears; for though the arbute shakes in the wind, the eye is lookless, and though the kelp has the acutest longing for the sea in it, the nose is stupid, and the dells and hard frith that are signs of the opaque substance of mortal will are dead dirt. There is a secret, porcine disgrace in loveless reading, just as there is in any instant of our lives when we are not remembering actively, and our passions are rubble and slain stones instead of the gems on Aaron's breastplate.

The comma and the circumflex have taken the place of a salubrious homely gnome, and subtle punctuation has become of greater weight than a potato and bread sentence. There are many tabu words in the Karl Marx, Wilde, Cocteau lexicon, like justice, morals, chaste, masculine, friendship and particularly heterosexual, which only a bumpkin writing fool would use, knowing that if he puts them into his book he will be called a sex blackguard by the members of the faith of Gomorrah, or a Rasputin reactionary by a high church Marxist. The criticaster is a dictionary savent, and though I was not canny enough to shun those index expurgatorious words, I am no man to sit like Lot at the gates of Sodom, but take flight into the mountains, for I have learned that the worst bleak crags and wilderness eagles are not so ravening as these humanity-lovers.

This scribbler is a very august and subtle speller and has given me some hard fisticuffs for being a Bottom the weaver at my lettering. First he calls me a pedant, which I am sure is his peacock skill at flattery, and a sign of his perverse intellect, because, despite their most piggish aberrations, our grammar-tradesmen seldom make mistakes in spelling. Other pedants would show them up right away if they did. His spleen is up because Michiavelli appeared in my book instead of Machiavelli, and he is a choleric and flighty wasp declaring that I write Mephistophilus for Mephistophiles, but should he look at the various Marlowe editions and Goethe translations he will find that Mephistophilus has three to four different ways of being lettered. Then I didn't spell eunuch the way he relishes it, for I put two n's in eunuch instead of one, to give this miserable word a kind of jocose priapic length. There is an old Greek saying that if you have no powers yourself, the onion, considered an aphrodisiac by the ancients, won't help you either. I admit it was folly to put that alphabetic onion in eunuch, and hereafter I shall go to the Delphic oracle and bother the gods not for self-knowledge, or socratic foolishness like that, but what I shall ask is, O Apollo, how do you spell Fool? and tell me, O Muse, whether Bacchus has passed a comma lately, or Silenus hiccupped a caesura?

He thinks I do not know that Apuleius wrote the *Golden Ass*, but imagines that I believe that the golden ass wrote Apuleius, o brazen ass! It has been the habit of the bursar Polonius in our colleges of lower learning to expose the ignorance of writers. I think it was Cotton who took the most oleaginous pleasure in telling the reader that Montaigne had put some words in the mouth of Ovid that Terence or Martial said, or that Robert Burton misquoted often. Who would be troubled about it except quibblers, since the citations are marvelous, no matter whose they are, and we get as prodigal a benefit from a wise remark that Burton said a Greek had written though it came out of a Latin verse. Besides, in the end, all sagacious homilies are anonymous, and those who pine for a little fame are simply trying to say what Seneca or Longinus wrote; if we are crafty we conceal our thefts entirely, but when we are a mirthful cut-purse Autolycus we just wink at those who find us out, and go on stealing from Shakespeare who cozened Plutarch whose *Lives* are a most noble cairn of literary thievery.

Herman Melville could not spell very well, and even in modern *Moby-Dick* texts the helmet of Mambrino is wrongly lettered; and in the *Encantadas*, that widowed lament of the soul which has already become a waste island for huge turtles and potherbs, he has failed to meet the dictionary requirements in the way he has shaped the word

Gallapagos. The *Billy Budd* Ms. was a grammar and punctuation bedlam also; but it is easy to find a page-proof reader to mend some of Melville's syntax, but where is there another man to write *Moby-Dick?*

THE MALICE OF WITLINGS

"Thou'rt sound in body; but some say thy mind
Envy doth ulcer; yet corrupted hearts
Such censurers must have."   Ben Jonson

One of the seven deadly sins of literature is a book review, which a writter requires. The dilemma of the writer perhaps is insurmountable. Seldom does a man of letters trouble over a real *boke*. Often our sacred memorabilia are decimated by an apprentice. Then there is the hack, and as the name implies, he saws the poet, as though he were the prophet Isaiah, into four quarters.

Then those who cannot write denounce those who can; or if someone happens to care for a collection of verse he is incapable of eulogizing it without proving that he knows far more than the author. How frequently does a poeticule fall upon, and in scurvy English, a sage who has committed a pair of solecisms or concern himself with the punctuation he deems improper.

It is not my intention to catalogue those who have sunk wisdom. However, there is *The Journal of Jules Renard*, Englished by the poet Louise Bogan, and Elizabeth Roget. It is an enchanting diary, and the language is clear and dear to the heart of any devotee of letters. Yet the venom of their assailant flowed copiously through his comments. "Thou sluggish spawn, that canst, but wilt not see! Feed on thyself for spight, and show thy kind:"— Ben Johnson. A steadfast biography about Ford Madox Ford, by Professor

Frank MacShane, was clawed by an olympian dwarf, who took up so much space quoting mixed metaphors and pelting flaws, it was difficult to find out, but not impossible, that the attack was made up of the most dreary and sluttish words . Doubtless there were mistakes in this very lengthy memoir, but what is important is that he excavated a whole period of literary culture with which most people are unfamiliar. Persons who cannot make a good book do not have sufficient understanding to realize it is impossible to compose a faultless one. Men are hopelessly frail, even writers and their executioners, and their errors come from their brains which are as weak as any other part of the body.

May nobody think I have the vapors and am in the dumps; what I allege to be the plight of the writer is asserted with jovian serenity. I never put together a shoal of vowels and consonants for mammon or for that other whore, fame. I propose to go along as I have always done, sowing dragon's teeth when necessary, and seeding affections in the souls of my unknown readers if I can. There is no nostrum, and the best I am able to do is to describe what happens, and let those who disagree with me read somebody else's errors.

Literature is politics, and the latter apart from the former, is demagogy. Balzac was called a statesman. Whatever justice there is in a people depends upon the purity of the diction employed by its seers. What then is the position of our literati? Are we a young nation already in its dotage?

Yesterday I looked at the *World-Telegram,* and at least ten of its pages were about the motion picture rabble, radio buffoons, and criminal and ruttish television programs. I glanced at its obituary notices; prominent attention was given to the deceased president of the clothing manufacturers, and to the director of women's shoe stores. There were less than four lines about Cecil Hemley, poet and novelist. I scarce knew this man, but should he have written one albic page he is worth more to America than millions of money-grubbers who do not care a whit for a great continent now loaded with absessed cities and deviscerated garage towns.

In one of the daily liberal rags there is a column, the Vermin's Nest, filled with gossip about vacuous stage people, a chatterbox in the town, or a millionaire roustabout, but never a hint of a savant.

There is no golden age of letters. In olden Thebes statues were erected to honor wrestlers and jugglers, but there was none to commemorate Pindar and his odes. That Anaxagoras, the Athenian cosmographer, wished to starve himself to death is rueful evidence that one century is as baneful as another. However, that Pericles importuned the desponding thinker to go on living for the sake of philosophy is a jubilant piece of history. When one Greek city-state was at war with a rival, the conquerors were so delighted with their captives who marched reciting hundreds of lines of Euripides that they freed them.

Jonathan Swift was the most potent figure in England for about four years, and it was not uncommon for a prime minister to hurry to the Dean's chambers to seek counsel before delivering an oration or framing a law. When the proprietor of a London bookstore informed Lord Bolingbroke that Robert Burton, who wrote the fantastical *Anatomy of Melancholy*, was standing only a few meters from him, the aristocrat came over to Burton and gave him a low bow.

Trash is our god, particularly if it is the latest novelty. One celebrated noddy of our times exclaims, make it new, but I say, make it human!

An Argentinian described the North American as a torpid and materialistic Caliban. How can we produce an Ariel, and at least, in small part, become a utopia of wise readers? Greed must not be our polestar, and though I detest any species of censorship, what are we to do about those who debauch the minds of a nation to acquire riches they cannot even use?

Is it impertinent to ask why J. Arthur Rank, the millionaire motion picture producer, bought most of the small bakeries in England? What can he do with more money? And what intelligent housewife can enjoy his sapless, hadean bread, wrapped in a windingsheet named cellophane? Recently a broadcasting company purchased a large publishing house. I cower as I ponder what will occur. The more caitiff factory fiction that is printed the fewer intelligent readers there will be in the land.

Does not every one owe as much to the republic as the colonial poet, Edward Taylor, or Thoreau, Emily Dickinson and Sherwood Anderson gave to it, and willing to be paupers and often anonymous in order to create the imponderabilia which are the health of its populace.

We live amidst vulgar products and none can escape the evil effects they have upon us. Handle a shoddy volume or stand eight hours rolling rubber tires down a noisome aisle, and who after that is not vacant and coarse? Let a man dote upon twelve sonnets and he will not be a drumbling fool in his amours. "Experience is in the fingers," said Thoreau.

How much longer can the American read pulp, fusty paperbacks, and listen to the commercial lullabies, those odious canticles sung to sell cleansing powders and mouth disinfectants, before we have a generation of simians ranging from the age of five to seventy.

Spite of the remarks I make regarding the poverty of

poets, let me add that the real mendicants are those who are ignorant. The point is not whether I can afford to be a writer, but can the citizens of the United States be emptied of all the thoughts we have inherited from the Nile, Babylon, the Tigris and Euphrates, and the old England that is now a corpse Hellas?

Since my youth I was zealous for erudition. It was not unusual for me to eat one meal a day in order to purchase a second-hand copy of Gissing's *By the Ionian Sea*, Tolstoi's *What is Art?* and Goncharov's *Oblomov*. A true writer is a learned reader. One wise man will conduct you to another and oleaginous fiction will increase your indolence. Petrarch confesses: "Augustine bade me search for Seneca *On Superstition*; Lactantius and many others made me desire the *Republic*; and Suetonius set me looking for the *Roman History* of Pliny." Moreover, many will tell you they desire to be a maker of poems but few are those who have enough character to resolve that they are going to study Plutarch, Tacitus and Propertius.

A very courteous young man, who lived on the same floor as I, said he had decided to be an author, but I saw he was spending his time and money on depraved prosers. One day, arguing with him over his lumpish and mouldy hours, and finding my admonitions were useless, I demanded he leave the room straightway, and not return until he became an exuberant bibliomaniac. He gazed at me with unimaginable astonishment; unable to understand why he was not sensible enough to depart, I realized I had requested him to quit his own apartment!

Across from my wizened flat was an older man who pined to be an artist, but who never did anything but gnaw the venetian blinds and bite his own soul. After a brief acquaintance, I insisted that he work, and he replied he could not because his walls were green. "In heaven's name," I expostulated, "paint them white." After my austere censure he explained he wanted to write. How perverse is the heart, and who can know it?

Let us go back to those who ravish our best quatrains and belles lettres. Every time shoaly doggerel is praised pensive verse is lost. How tiresome are the canting chimes of our pedantic journals on Henry James, Pound, Eliot, Lawrence, Gertrude Stein and Hemingway. One might imagine there had never been such figures as Theophrastus, Porphyry, Plotinus, Clement of Alexandria, Gavin Douglas, Samuel Daniel, Owen Felltham or La Bruyère. Who refers to Dekker's *Plague Pamphlets?* As one French critic said: "You can't find eight professional writers who have read Voltaire."

The cult of the same obtains in New York, Paris, Rome and Copenhagen. This creed is as detestable as the Marxists' St. Bartholomew's night when books that were not in agreement with Stalinist doctrines were slain. Has anything changed? Nowadays all one has to do is to announce that Pound or Fitzgerald is a basilisk to a reader and his next novel is thrown into limbo.

More than a decade ago I met somebody on *The New Yorker,* and after what I conceived to be a pleasant conversation, the reviewer said to me: "A man like you is a threat to me!"

Somewhat later a San Francisco versifier sent me three epistolary genuflexions telling me how much he admired *The Sorrows of Priapus*; he asked me whether I would give him a copy of it which I did. A number of months thereafter several thousand words, shrieking like the mandrake that has just been plucked, appeared in *Poetry* magazine divulging countless gargantuan defects of mine; my *admirer* stated

I did not understand life either. I met him in the Eighth Street Bookstore one day and after approaching him in the most friendly manner, I asked him, and without any squalid or hostile feelings, "Tell me, do you understand life?" to which he replied: "My God, no." Since I regard work far more noble than what people claim is uninterrupted every day ecstasy, I am unable to repress the temptation to cite the Comte de Villiers de l'Isle Adam: "And as for living, let us have our servants do that for us."

Years before the death of Sherwood Anderson, it was quite typical both of his adherents and adversaries to tell him that he was confused. There are many sophisms about clarity of emotion, but who has lucid moments except at rare intervals? Only bores have very clear minds, and how transparent they are. Bile is often mistaken for a panegyric; in the Goncourt *Journals* there is the following observation: "The greatest and most malignant conversational wit that Saint-Beuve possesses consists in tearing a man to pieces in the guise of defending him."

The quandaries are multitudinous. Myriads of trumpery wares come off the printing-presses every year, and what editor has the strength even to glance at a tithe of them. However, since so few books are worth his attention, why does pecuniary garbage receive the applause while literature remains a clandestine commodity?

I do not like to repeat the worn-out shibboleth, the freedom of the press, but is it a platitude to ask the columnist of sundry periodicals and papers, what do you propose to do with your liberty?

We deeply sympathize with a Russian whose opus is suppressed because he refuses to abide by the Communist Party line, but when our own memorable thoughts are not even noticed, what do we do about that? Whether a truth is hidden from readers for ideological reasons or a volume that does not give off a drowsy, opiate scent of money is inhumed, are we not censoring culture in the United States? Is it amiss to ask what would ancient Greece be without Anaximines, Eudoxus, Strabo, Aeschylus, Aristophanes, Anacreon and Simonides? Thoreau's *A Week on the Concord and the Merrimack* is our meal just as much as lentils and potatoes.

Isaac d'Israeli, the erudite father of the English prime minister, gives us some woeful records of the penury of the sacred citizens of his country. According to him, before the reign of George First, a dedication of a play to a lord or patron brought the author five to ten guineas. Stow, an antiquary, was so impecunious that he had to petition James I for a license to ask for alms. Look at the epistles of Erasmus; spite of his immense intellect, and though a familiar of the pope and kings, he constantly had to beg for money so that he could eat.

To come closer to our times ten copies of *Thus Spake Zarahustra* by Nietzsche and seventeen of Stendhal's *De l'Amour* were sold when they first issued. Christopher Smart's *Rejoice in the Lamb* was not found until two hundred years after the death of the poet. When it was brought out by Henry Holt in New York it was not even reviewed in this city, and over a period of thirteen years about 178 copies were sold.

The most obsidian hazard is the attempt to make a truthful book. What I mean by truth is words put together in a style that will delight the reader and whet his faculties.

The second peril for the writer is to wait for his work to be graved or given niggard attention. To those who consider what I have said extreme, let me refer to a droll encounter I had with Sherwood Anderson. Once he gave me a letter to friends of his in New Orleans in which he declared I had a brilliant but negative mind. After returning from the old creole quarter I had lunch with this marvelous populist singer of the midwest, and brought with me *The Note-Book of Sherwood Anderson*. Without telling him who had written it, I commenced to read aloud some of his own darksome lines about our cruel rubber and steel towns, pausing now and then after I had just finished a paragraph, to beseech him not to be too harsh with the author of such negations. He smiled sheepishly, and we parted from one another in the most affectionate manner.

Socrates always said he only was oracular as a denier, and Dryden felt he was worthless unless he was deriding something that was bad. Long ago I resolved to be, like Crates, a jocose iconoclast, to see whatever my eyes compelled me to regard without blinking the worst by calling it the best, and to accept my hindrances as the founts of any perceptions I may be lucky enough to discover.

STEPHEN CRANE : AMERICAN GENIUS

Stephen Crane was a New Jersey man, the son of an impecunious and plodding minister, but before he was twenty he wrote *Maggie, A Girl of the Streets*, published by himself. It is not a notable novel—and I say this in anticipation of the geniuses of the college textbooks who will inevitably give it to the students as a masterpiece.

I do not intend to offer the reader a shrewd analysis of *Maggie, The Red Badge of Courage,* "The Blue Hotel," or "The Open Boat." It is rather late for me or anybody else to appraise the talent of Stephen Crane. Everybody is reading notes, prefaces, and feuilletons on Melville, James, Poe, Dickinson, Dreiser, Norris, and Anderson, but how many are reading the books of these authors? Ford, Conrad, James, Hamlin Garland, and Sherwood Anderson said what there was to say about this gifted nature, and the only task ahead of the enthusiast of literature is to read Stephen Crane.

The sallow and emaciated Crane was the object of a great deal of clumsy and prurient newspaper gossip. The scandal consists of the fact that Stephen Crane met his wife in a house of ill fame in New Orleans, which is something that almost every author in the country has known for years. Since he was always writing about Wyoming saloon towns, Nevada mining gulches, or just plain Texas, his books gave ammunition to backbiters — and to New York patrolmen whose bullying Crane had reported to the police commissioner, Teddy Roosevelt. His marriage to a mistress of a New Orleans brothel did not help to abate villainous talk. Crane was not an alcoholic, nor was he debauched, but he was a latent consumptive. When he went to England some pseudo-friend let him have a dank medieval castle. The low spot where the moat had been was as malignant for a cough as a tarn in Poe's tales.

Stephen Crane believed in civility even though the sharp, rude gunfire phrases in "The Blue Hotel" proclaim him to have been the rough frontiersman in many ways. There was such a delicate subtlety in Crane's homage to older authors that he completely won Henry James and Joseph Conrad.

James lived close by the castle, and sent five unpublished manuscripts to Crane. It was a very gallant act, and a most discerning one. James, in many ways the most finical old maid of American letters, was a remarkable guesser. It took a novelist, a writing animal, to understand Crane, who had the head of a mettlesome horse that loves his master. Crane regarded anybody who cared for writing — James, Conrad, Ford — as his teacher. This does not mean that he was a humble ninny; as a matter of fact, Ford said Crane was always chastising him.

Crane was our pioneer terrain; he was Colorado, New Mexico, the mesquite, the Sierra Madre. With that pistol intelligence of his he took a fast sight on Mark Twain and said he could not stand four hundred pages of humor. He called Tolstoi's *War and Peace* "Peace and War," summing it up cleverly when he said it went on and on like Texas. Crane admired Tolstoi, but he had a poor regard for Zola, one of whose books may have been the reason for writing *The Red Badge of Courage*. Despite the acclaim *The Red Badge of Courage* has received, I think it is too preachy. It is far below the level of "The Blue Hotel," "The Open Boat," "The Bride Comes to Yellow Sky," or "The Five White Mice." Crane was hardly thirty when he died, and not a thinker. Our novel has been best when it is a simple celebration of American territory. Death Valley is what makes Frank Norris; Terra Haute is memorable in Theodore Dreiser and Sherwood Anderson is Ohio ground.

Everyone has written bad stories or novels. Melville said there is a great deal of trash in genius. It is foolish to assume that Crane has perished because some, or even many, of his narratives were rubbish. Human beings die many times, and the more original they are the more true this is. It is crude bombast to think that anybody can tell whether Crane would have developed had he lived. No one knows, and since self-knowledge is so meager in the wisest and best of men, it is doubtful that Crane could have foretold his own powers.

Yet what honest, vigorous words this "uneducated" author had! This consumptive had energy; Aristotle says a poet is an enthusiastic nature which one will never find in our academic dumps.

Ford wrote: "Poor, frail Steevie, in the little room over the porch in the E, writing incessantly — like a spider that gave its entrails to nourish a wilderness of parasites.... I wonder which is the better mode of life for a writer — of the two modes followed by those two Americans in that old corner... There was James with his carefully calculated life in a Georgian treasure house — with his lawns and his Ladies and his flowers and his old, mellow, brick garden walls and his smooth-running household — and all his suavities... And with all his passionate inner life for ever concealed so that you would have sworn he had never lived at all .... And there was Crane, for ever stuffed in somewhere as waste paper is stuffed into any old drawer — in an Oxted villa; on a Cuban hillside; in a hut in Tin Can, Nevada; in an Athens hospital; in an Adirondack tent; in a

New York rooming-house; in an open boat; in an Elizabethan manor — and in a grave in Elizabeth, New Jersey, of
all places in the world to have chosen for you . . ."

MID-AMERICAN CHANTS : SHERWOOD ANDERSON

Sherwood Anderson has left us his *Mid-American Chants* which few have read. Most of our best volumes are odd, little curios which we hoard in our parnassian attic. Who talks about Sherwood Anderson's *Many Marriages, Poor White, Triumph of the Egg,* the late Haniel Long's chapbook on the sorrows of Cabeza de Vaca, or William Carlos Williams' *In the American Grain?* — all honey in the carcass of the lion. You cannot find such sweetness in our modern sheep of literature.

I remember when Anderson, in many respects a renowned obscurian in his own day, wrote that when he met people they asked him his name, and after he had told them, they replied: "Oh, you're the famous Maxwell Anderson!" to which he timidly answered: "No, I'm just Sherwood Anderson." To lump these two names together is profane, and it is the sort of scurrile newspaper nihilism that passes for literary criticism today. Anderson was often abused by almost every 'mewing' critic because he naively admitted that he was confused, and had no clear knowledge of what he was doing or had written. He who tells you he understands life is himself dead rather than quick. And he who imagines that he is far more reasonable than he is automatic can never make a book that is not a heap of dross. Sherwood Anderson's poems and novels are among the most enchanting reveries and *unreasonable* dreams to be found in our meager brooks of Helicon. It is hard enough to compose a rural hymn, but what a plague it is to put one's trembling pulses into the musty hands of scribblers and dogmatic and flippant reviewers. Let me cite honest old Dekker who knew the sorrow of placing true, good words in their proper order, and who was immensely underestimated by so many of his contemporaries, even by the great Ben Jonson who collaborated with him: "For he that dares hazard a pressing to death (thats to say, To *be a man in print*) must make account that he shall stand (like the old Wethercock over Powles Steeple) to be beaten with all stormes."

We are now in the long, cold night of literature, and most of the poems are composed in the Barren Grounds.

When this Ohio skald began to write, he had almost no guides; poets need wise predecessors who can nourish them. But what viatcum could there be for him in such skulled pamphlets as *Good Newes from Virginia* or *The Simple Cobbler of Aggawam?* The colonial planters had converted the new land into a theocratic Golgotha.

Sherwood Anderson could derive much comfort and learning of the heart from Henry David Thoreau, a great man in any country, but even he was too much of an aerial seer for this carnal bard.

There were the local-color writers who had influenced Dreiser: Fuller's *Cliff-Dwellers* and *With the Procession*, novels about Chicago, and Edgar Howe, the sage of Potato Hill and the author of *The Story of a Country Town*, which may have been in Anderson's mind when he began *Winesburg, Ohio*. Without any inclination to belittle these craftsmen of our lonely, midland landscape, they were sentient terrain rather than savants. Stendhal has said of his own age: "This generation has nothing to continue; but everything to create."

I have read these *Chants* for over thirty-five years, and they are like birds treading the spirit until it flutters.

Anderson delighted in common similitudes that would

recall his hearers to the old bucolic life he cherished. He said: "I'm an empty barrel floating in the stream;" and "Out of the mud at the river's edge I moulded myself."

He was an unaffected, artless singer, a mid-western child of the Muses, and much of his village music seems easy to imitate or to make, and so do the sentences in Henry David Thoreau's *A Week on the Concord and the Merrimack Rivers:* "The remains of Indian weirs, made of large stones, are still to be seen in the Winnipiseogee, one of the headwaters of this river." Would to God it were so simple to do, for then think how many Thoreaus and Sherwood Andersons we would have!

And elsewhere Anderson goes on with his chant: "I was suckled face downwards;" he was not speaking of his own nature as of those whose faces are turned awry or hindward and who showed their backs when they greeted others.

In another place he says, "Pshaw;" and I can still hear him saying it in that accent of his so like the cawing of a crow in a field, and I wish he were here now even if he said nothing else.

" . . . Pshaw . . . let me alone, Keokuk, Tennessee, Michigan, Chicago, Kalamazoo — don't the names in this country make you fairly drunk?"

He knew that people were bread eaten by the Machine, and he wondered: "Can a singer arise and sing in this smoke and grime?" Though he half-believed we were all "like the sewerage of our towns," he did not sit in the Cloaca when he wanted to make a song, but on the Sibyl's Stone.

OSCAR WILDE: THE SIN OF PARADOX

Oscar Wilde was a Greek boy, and we should look at his life as an Athenian fable. He was punished for a vice that was as much part of the habit and dress of Attica as were the wallet and the holes in the cloak of the Cynic philosophers. What doomed Wilde long before his imprisonment in Reading Gaol was his pursuit of pleasure, a plague and snare for everybody. There was one pupil of Socrates who said that he would rather go mad than feel pleasure. Wilde's real weakness was that he did not dread what so attracted him. Well, Pascal said that no man can fear himself enough.

De Profundis was first published in 1905 which was a few years after the death of Wilde. This was an incomplete text consisting of letters written by Wilde in Reading Gaol to Lord Alfred Douglas. One wonders whether these letters, far from hindering appetite, may not kindle it. The early pages of the book are a vexsome and lachrymal account of Wilde's financial misfortunes. Wilde writes that he spent more than five thousand pounds in two years on Lord Douglas's dinners, travels, flowers; and these epistles read like a debauched supper described by Petronius. Douglas was a wastrel with a mean poetaster's talent, and though Wilde's acrimonious judgments of him are true, they are not the result of wisdom. Wilde had no palate for morals.

Wilde tells us how the scandal was started. As long as the Irish wit was the idolized flaneur of London he made no account of his evil reputation. When the father of Douglas accused Wilde of having seduced his son, Wilde brought charges against the elder. It was Wilde's most puerile error.

He should never have gone to the law, but should have left for Paris instead. Moreover, he should have hidden his vice. Everyone has some skulking disgrace that has cindered his soul, as we know from the hinted shames in the Sonnets. What man can least bear of all his miseries is the ruin of his name, which is something to which Wilde paid little heed until he was broken by the public tongue. Douglas's father had boasted at his club that nothing in his life had given him such satisfaction as putting Wilde in prison. The father was the rough, mediocre Philistine so often delineated by Shaw, himself a witling of Gaza. As for the young, flowerlike Douglas, he was a seasoned artist of debauchery in which Wilde was just the ingenue.

Wilde relates how the crowds at the railroad station simpered at him; he was standing between two policemen, handcuffed and with bowed head. The propensity to jeer is an unlovely and almost universal human failing, and from this moment *De Profundis* is our own yoke. We watch as Oscar Wilde turns to the Gospels; each day he reads the New Testament in Greek. His mother has died and the law, as he writes, has taken from him his two children. When he hears this he falls to his knees and cries out with some obscure pain in him that the body of the Lord is the body of a child. After many months in Reading Gaol the doctor allows Wilde to have white bread instead of the ordinary brown prison loaf. For the first time in his life he has tasted bread of the poor and the hungry. He gathers up all of the white crumbs, adding with the naive trembling which comes over men who have had some terrible suffering that he ate the remaining morsels because he did not wish to waste them. This was possibly one of Wilde's few chaste remarks, but it is a lie.

Wilde was by nature and mind perverse; he thought that

beautiful lies are art. This is wit, but not the truth, and paradox is a sin because the man that utters it is more interested in pleasing and amusing than in writing what is good or just. Cicero was very acute when he wrote that in Epicurus, the philosopher of pleasure, such words as good and evil and justice are not to be found. We are likely to believe that he received some benefits from Reading Gaol. True, he sat in shame. Wilde was also penitent; but it is an enigma that a froward man shall repent but remains steadfast in his errors.

André Gide writes of Wilde after his release from Reading Gaol; Wilde took the name of Sebastian Melmoth and he resided in an obscure village in the neighborhood of Dieppe. Wilde had left prison with a high motive and wanted to write one beautiful book to "rob malice of its venom, and cowardice of its sneer..." But he was torn to pieces; he looked like a bloated Nero with his rotten stumps of teeth and corrupt skin, and he wore on one of his fingers a ring with the setting of an Egyptian scarab in lapis lazuli. He was a fallen dandy, a rouged fop, with the prayers of Golgotha on his lips.

Wilde has always been in some ways Gide's master. What did he teach? In his little book Gide writes that Wilde told him that art does not hurt people. Gide then retells one of Wilde's New Testament fairy tales...Jesus returns to Nazareth which is no longer a humble village of fishers, but a Greek town of nard, honey, white roses and slaves. He sees a familiar man in long, disheveled tresses, smelling of wantonness, and sorrowfully asks him why he led such a dissolute life and the man replies: "I was a leper — Thou hast healed me." Wilde also said, "To regret one's own experience is to arrest one's own development." It is a clever remark and one has to give it very close thought to see how wrong it is.

67

Wilde perverted the New Testament no less than Gide, his disciple, garbled old Greek fables. Gide says that Wilde told him that his lips were too straight to be artistic. Evidently Gide accepted the words of his hedonistic mentor, for his *Theseus* is a piece of intellectual perversion. In his rendering of the ancient legend, Theseus's infamy is his shallowness; Theseus's hatred of his father is the malice of a modiste, and Pasiphæ's passion for the bull, which was tragic to the ancient poets, is vaudeville lechery.

Gide writes with such artless simplicity that the reader is likely to forget that he is not reading Matthew's but Caligula's Gospel. Gide says that Wilde had told him after he had left prison that he had given his genius to his life and his talent to his writing. It is a pathetic epigram — something like the gargoyles on great cathedrals, which do not represent terrible sins any more than Wilde's remark indicates insight. Wilde thought he had to be waggish to the last. Christ, as Wilde writes in *De Profundis*, compares the soul to the smallest cummin seed. Man's folly is that he does not know that his brain is much smaller than his soul; for how few have enough judgment to know that the mind is absolutely helpless and wicked without the spirit.

THE TRUE NIETZSCHE

Friedrich Nietzsche, the Bacchic philosopher of energy and dark sayings, has been mutilated more than any other great modern thinker. It has been common to revile him as the proto-Nazi, an anti-Semite and a statist. In a period of mounting anti-Semitism, in which a dying world must find some helpless minority people as the usual ritual bull to dismember, it is very important to understand Nietzsche. Was this seer, who had such a deep influence upon romantic natures like Georg Brandes, Thomas Mann and Emma Goldman, a muscle-and-war Wotan or Thor, playing, long after his death, the Jew-baiting satyr in a *Walpurgisnacht* that has by no means ended? The answer is "no." Nietzsche's works must be taken out of villainous hands, and Walter Kaufmann, the author of *Nietzsche*, has performed a considerable service in this respect alone. His *Nietzsche* should relieve many ardent but troubled admirers of *Thus Spake Zarathustra*.

Nietzsche's brief, but torn, life can be divided into three parts. At twenty-four years of age he was a brilliant philology professor at the University of Basel. But with no mind to be a college philosopher, he wrote a heterodoxical book on æsthetics, *The Birth of Tragedy* (1872). He had the greatest reverence for Greek learning and already considered himself a Socratic nature. After ten years as a lecturer, he resigned because of ill health. He left the university for the same reasons that he relinquished his enthusiastic friendship with Richard Wagner — soul-sickness. Nietzsche, who had said that his own youth would have been unendurable without Wagner's music, had such an aversion for the composer in the role of the Teutonic prophet that he could no longer go to his home. Whenever Richard or Cosima Wagner sent him an invitation, he got migraine headaches and even vomited. The anti-Wagnerian phase was the beginning of the second part of the life of this Alpine mountain sage who wanted to be twenty thousand leagues above humanity, Junker mankind in particular.

But the most significant portion of Nietzsche's life is the third, that of his madness, for it was at this time that he became famous, and oh, what infamy there is in this prostitute, Renown, especially Nietzsche's! Up till the time of his insanity, he had been basely neglected; so little heed was paid to the first three sections of *Zarathustra* that he considered it futile to write or to print the last part. Then a terrible irony occurred. Nietzsche became known through his sister, Frau Forster, who had married in 1885 Dr. Bernard Forster, organizer of an anti-Semitic colony in Paraguay called Germania Nueva!

This marriage agitated Nietzsche a good deal and gave him those queasy feelings that often tell people much more than their minds do. Dr. Forster had already been involved in some unsavory street-car incidents in which Jews were roughly handled. Forster was one of those typical, unlearned Herr Doktors with which Germany and our own land is so unhappily glutted. Despite all the babble about German culture, Nietzsche had written that after the death of Goethe there were no more than four gifted writers in the country, Schopenhauer, Heine, Lessing and Nietzsche. Lessing, a beautiful nature and the author of one of the most noble books of criticism, *The Laocoön*, had said more or less the same things about German poetry and civilization. It must be remembered that Lessing's friendship for Moses

Mendelssohn, the Jewish philosopher, was considered an act of social courage; and that Heinrich Heine had found the German professional and writing classes so hostile that he lived almost all of his life as an exile in Paris. What Hitler later regarded as Jewish corrosive wit, the Heinesque doubt, was just as abhorrent to the average academic in Heine's time. Dante, one of the greatest of the world's believers, had written: "I love to doubt as well as to know."

We see, then, how sterile were the educated classes in Germany, and also how pessimistic; for otherwise how could so negligible a population of Jews as there was in Germany be regarded as a menace to the nation? The German fear of a few hundred thousand Jews was the expression of a gross professional mind incapable of intellectual appetite or vision.

In 1870 anti-Semitism was officially organized in Germany, so that the period was ripe for the Wagnerian propaganda which Dr. Forster was peddling. This poltroon did not even have a first-hand knowledge of Wagner's musty intellectual goods or of the composer's militant vegetarianism, which Hitler later adopted to show the German people how to be content on a Third Reich vegetable plate. Then there was Wagner's dreamy idealism of the antivivisectionist that had a remarkable appeal for the Forsters as well as for the sinewy Siegfried anti-semite. (Both Wagner and Hitler were themselves very small and droll Siegfrieds.)

Germania Nueva in Paraguay soon collapsed. The colonists accused the Forsters of swindling them, and Forster took his own life. The widow returned to Germany to take care of her stricken brother. Mr. Kaufmann writes: "The tragedy was played out ... and a satyr play followed."

Nietzsche had watched from a distance Wagner's efforts to establish Bayreuth as the Holy City of anti-Semites; this attempt to elevate Bayreuth Nietzsche called "cultural philistinism." He had criticized Kant because he "clung to the university, submitted to governments"; he had condemned Hegel for writing, "The State is the actuality of the ethical ideal"; and he had the sharpest contempt for the serving-maid in Luther, who had said: "If they take from us body, goods, honor, child, and wife: let it go — the Reich yet remains to us!" He denounced race politics, another word for Jew-baiting, calling himself a "good European," an "anti-anti-Semite," and he showed the plainest abomination for what he called the "extirpation of the German spirit in favor of the German Reich." In a letter to Overbeck he said "... there is a special anti-Semitic interpretation of *(Zarathustra)* which makes me laugh very much." Nothing helped; the anti-Jewish *Parteigenossen* presented him to the public as a Teuton *Politiker*.

It had been a great sacrifice for Nietzsche to relinquish Wagner's friendship. In *Zarathustra* he wrote: "What does he know of love who did not have to despise just what he loved!" He had loved Wagner and had a secret, Dionysiac passion for Cosima Wagner, the illegitimate daughter of Franz Liszt. He was a very lonely genius and not particularly lucky with women. There was a Fraulein Lou Salome, a disciple of his thinking; he hoped she would become his wife. She later wrote a book about him instead, marrying another author of much less artistic worth than Nietzsche.

The migraine headaches worsened despite the invigorating Alpine walks. This sick man was an apostle of health, and mountain-mind climbing is characteristic of all his remarkable books. By 1889 the poor mind was lost; Nietzsche was living in that grubby factory city, Turin, in hilly Piedmont, when he had his first fit of madness. Cesare Lombroso, author of *Genius and Insanity*, was also living in

Turin at the time of Nietzsche's collapse. Nietzsche saw a rough coachman flogging a horse, and he fell, his arms flung around the horse's neck! He was taken to the clinic at Jena and then removed to the asylum for the insane. His friend, Overbeck, who came to help him, would never repeat what he referred to only as the Dionysiac mutterings of Nietzsche, already as mad as Ophelia cheeping bawdy valentine verse. The lunatic Nietzsche sent out notes to friends, signing himself as the Greek god of wine; one scrawl he posted to Cosima Wagner addressed her as Ariadne and called himself Dionysus.

Mr. Kaufmann writes that Frau Forster had gained the exclusive right to all of her helpless brother's works; and here the comedy and the deluxe fraud begin. What intellect had Frau Forster for her noble task? Mr. Kaufmann tells us that she asked Rudolf Steiner, a Goethe scholar, "for lessons in her brother's doctrine." She published almost every year his "collected works," suppressing anti-teutonic maxims or epigrams; finally she patched together thousands of random and disparate jottings and scribblings and issued them under the misleading title of *The Will to Power*.

Charlatans had always gathered around Nietzsche, causing people to ask whether he was not himself a quacksalver as well as homosexual. There was Doctor Schuler who promised to cure Nietzsche through a Corybantic male dance; Schuler had looked up ancient texts to find the suitable armour the youths should wear in the cultic dance which was to heal the great, hurt mind.

The madness made many query Nietzsche's worth. But the sages that have had the profoundest influence upon our age have been deformed or crazy or tubercular; paradoxically, their works have had enormous intellectual force and sanity. Kierkegaard was crippled; Hölderlin, the German mystic poet, was out of his mind; Schiller was consumptive, and our own Randolph Bourne was a miserable little hunchback.

What does Nietzsche teach? There are more parables crannied in that eagle's eyrie than can be put down in this essay. In an age of desperado inertia, weak in character, he shows us that in great willing is art and morality. What is important is to ascend the moral mountains, and though we roll down each time from the summit like the Sisyphean rock, it is our will to return that is Vision. Or to speak after the manner of Zarathustra, let us say, "It is my striving that is my Temptation."

We have made language so common that we have ceased to be symbolic readers. Unless we examine the total intellect of the poet as his text we shall misinterpret Blake or Shakespeare just as foolishly as Nietzsche has been distorted.

It seems that our task today is to save our savants from the disgrace the mediocre heart would heap upon them. Nietzsche paid very dearly for the ideas that he has bequeathed to us. It may be that the solitude he required for his apothegms drove him mad; perhaps he craved insanity; what other physic had he? Socrates took the hemlock, to perpetuate his ideas. Miserable irony; but no matter, he was a monarch of the spirit, and if we ourselves are moral and desperate readers, we can find in every book that Nietzsche wrote the hard alpine stuff for our wills. The great Goethe said, "Who overcomes himself, his freedom finds."

METHUSELAH'S FUNERAL

"Whatsoever goeth upon his paws, among all manner of beasts that go on all four, these are unclean ... among the creeping things that creep upon the earth; the Weasel, and the Mouse, and the Tortoise, ... the Ferret, and the Chameleon, and the Lizard, and the Snail, and the Mole." LEVITICUS

"Let Hashum bless with the Fly, whose health is the honey of the air ... Let Malchia bless with the Bat ... Let Hagar rejoice with Gneison, ... the eagle ... Let Rebekah rejoice with Lynx ... Let Jamin rejoice with the Bittern blessed by the name of Jesus for ... the draining of the fens."
A SONG FROM BEDLAM, by Christopher Smart

"When one of these animals (cats) dies they wrap it in linen and then, wailing and beating their breasts, carry it off to be embalmed; and after it has been treated with cedar oil and such spices as have the quality of imparting a pleasant odour and of preserving the body for a long time, they lay it away in a consecrated tomb." Diodorus Siculus

This is the book of the Cat Sin which was written by the cat men and women of New Topeth, an island village that lies in the sand dunes of Hinnom. These are Ham's descendants of whom it is told, idleness begat sloth, which produced malice that begat the Cat Sin. What issue has Cat Adam? Adam bare Seth who married his Angora sister, and they bare Maltese-Angora Enoch.

75

These are an old people with Hebrew names whose vices are antique. It is reported that the delicate men that knocked on Lot's door, demanding the release of the two male angels, came with cats and dogs whose tails they stroked, and they bit their ears into which they neighed the most amorous vows. They broke the Mosaic tablets, called themselves the Cat Nazareths, were great wine-drinkers, ate corrupt bread, and affected the cropped head and foreskin of the people of Gaza.

They erected cat and dog temples of Nineveh brick, and built animal cemeteries that were astonishing as the walls of Erech. They ornamented these brutes with golden trinkets, and silver neckware, and laced their legs with onyx, beryl, and jasper, and pruned their nails. In winter they covered the beasts in wool, and the cat slept on the pillow, and they loved them more than the drops of honey from the courtesan's mouth. When a cat or dog died, they sorely wept and mummified his remains, giving as homage molten images of mice and hemorrhoids, the Philistine custom.

The Cat Nazareths of Ham were a confusion and a fear to their circumcised kin whom they slew; for they detested the sheep, the he-goat, the ram, and the cote, saying, "Look, Circumcised Shephard, upon my tender cat flock; what do you know of the honey and the riddle of pleasure; come into the feline cote, fool." Their kin fled to the bald Carmel peak, or sought refuge in ravine solitude, and they concealed their sons; for the sin of Ham is in every man, and every one must guard against it as Shem and Japeth did by going backwards toward their father Noah to cover his nakedness.

In the Old Scripture it is written, In the beginning was the FATHER, but in the Cat Testament, it is, "I shall set my mother against my father, and he shall be her chattel, and she shall marry again though he live, and the mother shall

76

rule the house, and the step-father shall be her maid, and her son shall be a man who shakes his hunkers as he walks."

The Islander is of Asian origin, and his curried vice sticks out in his long, but vacant Sumerian nose. His main occupation is sloth, although he is a clam-digger, and does some cat-trading. He has a cat-cemetery, and he buries animals in the same graveyard with his mother and father. It is hard to know whether it is a Siamese or a father that lies beneath a scrub-pine cross or a cement-block slab. The epitaphs are also misleading, for the grief inscribed in tender words on the headstones would awaken the most apathetic heart. "Here lies my baby, Samuel Shad, born April 12, 1935, who lived but four years, dying of gout; I overfed him, Jesus spare me."

"This is the tomb of Timothy M., who ate too many moths, but who was good as the Apostle for whom he was named. Selah."

"Jacob Stotebury, Jan 4, 1867, d. Mar 2, 1929, R.I.P."

"This is my Sister, Cherub Rahab, may she have happiness in Canaan, and may I be buried at her side, my hand in hers."

The Islander attends Cat Mass at Our Stucco Lady of the Alley; his beast laws and dog scriptures go as far back as the wild practices of the Sabeans, neighbors of ancient Israel, who recited a secret feline hymeneal when they grafted fruits, forcing the Sabean apple to gender with the pear. Mating the apricot with the peach, mixing linen with wool, was considered sodomy among the ancient Jews, for it creates lawless confusion and madness.

The Islander has double dreams; everything heats his double mind which is male and female; unspeakable images of a gnat boiling for a louse, a grasshopper mingling with a toad, a pebble with a jellyfish, a bee stinging a porpoise's ear. Lying, deceit and indolence are like a mud-ditch or the mouse-colored fungus. They care for the pismire, and groan for the lickerish bat. They eat the owl, the crow, and the snail to inflame them. Falsehoods give them no less happiness than putrid pools and the kite, and they bosom their malice which is a stinging spider that sucks upon the flesh. What is loathsome is better than truth because it kindles the skin; for they steal and smell and simper for skin-itch.

The Islander admires what astonishes the mountain and the cloud, the eagle in its misty eyrie, the swan that pleasures the eye, and the heron plucking the solitary waters of a cove, but is not the eagle a wounder, the swan a Judas among the birds, and the heron unclean?

The inhabitants of New Topeth do not lose their hair which is dry bird feathers; and the Methuselah, Enos and Seth in the Hinnom sands live long enough to deceive all mankind. The reason for their longevity is that they partake of the sap of the malignant scrub-pine, a tree that fills aliens with misgivings and desolation, sea-salt, and kelp. Hypocrisy prolongs life, and eases wicked bowels just as truth-seeking wears men out. There is some brew from long sleep and dead salt places which makes men live for a century.

These people dwell in shacks on the sand hills, or in vales overrun with lizards, sour grass, and they dig the clam or open scallops; grow the melon, radish and lettuce on loam that is mostly powdered rock, sand, weeds, and weasel dung. "Cursed be the hoe, the rake, the hammer and the mattock," says the Islander, giving thanks to the wild beach plums, the berries and sumac and the nettle that grow without toil.

The adam's apple shows against the neck of the Islander like a secret shame. He pays his vows to the hunchback tree, to the earth-devouring pine, and to the birch, the false holy ghost of the forest. Having great skill in ecstasies he weds to hide his habit, marrying niggard women with February coffin chins, and he secretes them in gullies or huts leaning upon sand-crannies. Men and women are never seen together at New Topeth except in the dog-shearing season or at cat exequies.

He praises the moon which is a cat planet, but he abominates the ocean, and his prayer is a lunar cat liturgy for the deceased and this is the funeral text:

Remember Siamese Amalek who had a Gentile Foreskin, and whose double paw was bruised by the adder.

Balaam was a Cape Cod Tiger, and the Shepherd of my cellar; he was the Bull of the pusses, may he feed and gender forever in Paradise.

Let Joseph, who has a coat of many colors, and who died senile in the grain and feed store, lie on hay and straw in Christ's Bosom.

Let my cat Job, who was never house-broken, and who expired at the Orleans Animal Rescue Society, find peace in Jesus's Animal Rescue in heaven. Amen.

Praised be Sampson, the potent, who sustained a horrible scab from a Provincetown beast and who died of scallop poison.

Blessed be the name of Ham of New Topeth, for Mouse Pond, Racoon Lagoon, Truro, Highland Lights, and the Provincetown wharves that supplied Abigail with flounder and mackerel.

Let Gideon, that made his bed upon the gypsy-moths in the apple branches, rejoice upon the Mole, the Lizard, the Frog in the Spirit Realms, and may the Christmas pudding cooked by Pharaoh's baker be his meal. Gideon, the alleycat was the buckler of my kitchen.

Lament for Moses, a Tiger, who fell upon my open

shears, and whose remains lie in dog-town; let the slab I purchased for him at the Hyannis monumental yards comfort his soul.

Pray for Persian Barabbas who stole boiled beans from the oven when the door was ajar; though we drank porridge from the same bowl he was never corrected till wicked Abimilech, my neighbor, cast a lead-pipe at his skull. Amen.

Let Nabal, Abimilech's brute, that is a wine-sot, and drinketh up all the kerosene from the barrel, know the sorrow of swamp-grass and fleas, and then be shriven.

Weep for Hagar, my Ishmaelite Maltese, who slew single-footed five robins from Brewster and Dennis.

Thank heaven for fat Jeshurum, may the ground he tread be hallowed, for he made his ordure in secret places.

Lament for Yankee Tabby Nimrod, the mighty hunter, who never impoverished the cupboard, for the toad, the fieldmouse, and the weasel were always with him. The Lord and the Weasel be praised.

Let Ahab, who expired of the Neapolitan disease, but who held his tail erect in his prime, be recollected forever.

Let Caleb, the lion of Judah, find the peace in Mount Zion that the Philistine dogs denied him in his own yard, be a companion of the Archangel Michael.

Cursed be Abimilech and the Finnish washerwoman, Annah Malchus, for her hair is a horse tail, and she stole Methuselah who died from Finnish black bread and the clams in her woodshed. Hallelujah.

THE GARMENT OF RA

I

The voice of the rains cannot find the rivers,
The leaves are orphaned by thrush and crane,
The hills cannot foal;
The foot plagues the lily and the moss
When it treads upon their cry unheard.
The cured leper is one cubit less in compassion.
The doctor of knowledge is the cripple of Bethesda,
The jaw of Peter is the rock of salvation,
But not a tare scuds in the gutter
For the Moabite Ruth or the mouth of Lazarus.
The eyes that are wheels sin in every place.
The coptic frog is fertile, the womb of Abigail has failed,
The beetle is prolific, the Shulamite is sere,
The olive in the cold hills is barren Hannah,
The mandrakes of Haran cannot tempt Jacob;
Gad, Reuben and Manasseh are unable:
Sleep is the broken pitcher of Sodom,
The hermaphrodite stands before the couch,
Lot cannot bolt the door of the dream.

II

The first mortals were content in swamp and reed,
Herbs of the marsh and dog's toothgrass were bread;
The Kosmos was man's constant God and parent,

81

There was no sorrow or pain in the hollow knees,
Sidon and murex and Arabic alabaster were unknown.
The seasons were no more than a matter of winds.
In a secret lair lurked the hour
Lest she be taken in the weir.
The day was a timorous deer asylumed in a gorge.
Pomp was the feather of the heron.

Men were plant and the cowries of the shore,
Woman a potherb, her legs and hair were rain.
River-rushes, fennel stalk, the dusk
Were the odors of apples and desire,
Sea-weed and nettles yoked the buds and stems.
When Sirius raised his pinions
The Nile mothered the cucumbers, the melons and the leeks.

Salt-pools were the eyes and head of man,
His vertebra, a tidal seam;
The marshes dreamed, the dunes thought,
The Ocean, swamp and sands were in his mind and visage;
He had no wish to grasp them
Because he had no feet or hands,
The malign tutors of greed and strife.
The small stones slept near him as lambs.
Sea and quagmire, kelp and cockle
Were mother and father, and Abel who is feeling.
Of the salt-deeps are the sages,
Adam, Moses, Plato were sea-dolphins;
Cow, mule, ox were house and custom.
Palm-wine is for age and burial,
Of salt is the intellect of Uriel,
Christ spoke Aramaic, a littoral tongue.

The first words grew unsown in bogs,
Where Isis was the mourning hawk for Osiris.
In the salt delta Thoth was clad in papyrus,
The plant of the alphabet and the god Hermes.
Thoth is Hermes, the water of death.
Papyrus is the raiment of the books of Rā,
And the steadfast garment of the mummy.
Flax and hemp desert Orpheus and Musæus,
Palm-leaves stray from the holy Rig-Veda,
Sabine linen forsakes Romulus and Numa;
Of the skin of the he-goat was parchment,
Is this the tunic of Thales and Solon?

III

The almond increases the greed of Solomon;
The date-palm is the courtesan's tree.
Jerusalem's fig is the fruit of Ishtar.
The Shulamite is the dove of Moloch.
The sycamore and acacia are vain Sardanapalus.
The apple and wine-press are Gaza's snare;
But of cockle and desert was Enos.
Sow soft fruits in crabbed weather,
Etesian winds roughen the furrow of the olive,
Fir, hemlock and the yew are mountain wood,
Dour are their leaves;
These are no treason's summer friends.
Gall-oak, sea-bark, hilly ash and poplar
Were the names of deities and hewn tree-men.
Wild branches show their maiden buds earliest
When their trunks are tripods in the marshes.
Hills and winds guard the manna-ash.

Soft zephyrs on the stony mesa
Enliven the alder and recollection.
The chestnut is a Cato on bleakest knolls;
Elm is of the hardest pith on wintry slopes.
Forest is the hope of the disciples;
More learned than the fig is wildest ground.

The Essene thrives on gall and alum.
Vetch, fenugreek and chaff are frugal fellows,
Manna is the bread of the sandy Tarfa bush.
The turnip grows strong in a cold bed,
A poultice of lupine for healing lust,
And lentil humbles error.
Thyme and the mutinous berry of the Kermes-Oak
Restore the loveless eye.
Wheat is a moiety of the holy body of God;
Timothy is more steadfast than the son,
And mustard-seed sturdier than a brother's oath.
Bracken and fennel remember their roots;
Autumn is as stacte pounded in a mortar.
Sadness is a pleasant scent in the nose,
Grief is a writ on the lips of grape.

When the pistachio can scarce bud,
And the barley no longer stalk and ear,
And the yeoman bean has been quenched,
Can Solon cure decay?

                    IV

I marveled at the alphabet of Thoth,
The footprints of gulls were Aramaic inscriptions

For Christ and the twelve Apostles.
Papyrus, immune from the crocodile's jaw,
Was lonely river-grass at Elephantine.
Isis in quest of Osiris sailed in a wicker-boat,
John the Baptist journeyed on the Nile in osier.
The plant of knowledge was not flesh or season;
Etesian gusts or Arcturus was not its bane.
I girded my blood in the garment of Rā,
Naked Semiramis was my Talmudic lore,
Her Tyrian skirts and crisping-pins were Cabbala.
Dying was for buxom geese and a dotard's fable.

V

Fire is prophecy, water is dream,
And Ishtar is summer desire.

Blood is wild and unsecret in the sun;
The Ocean contents the briny calves,
The Nile is a lotus-couch for the river-horse,
And the nuptial mud of the crocodile.
The senses pipe ninny songs to dotards of balsam.
Pan goes with a pipe to the holy mountain
Seeking a bosky place for his fornications.
Eve is osier and appetite,
And three seasons round as Thoth decreed.
Her clothes were axe-weed and parsley.
The shoe of Boaz is the marriage-ring of Ruth.
The ten fingers of the hands are for the laws of Moses,
The toes of Delilah are the pleasures of Gaza.
An orbed forehead is the amulet of Venus,
The small foot is a Phoenician coxcomb,
But a sign of the weak bridegroom.

The apple and cedar are vain and amorous,
The doves of Astarte nest in Absalom's branches,
The yew is the tree of Bacchus.
The Lusitanian mare is an Epicurus of touch,
The thistles of Havilah are Adam's portion.
Man is the ruin of Ocean, behemoth and worm.
Are all who breathe the winds illicit?
The joys that are not eaten have no lees.
An acacia in the necropolis gladdens an epitaph,
Virgins flourish without wantonness in the tomb.
The sepulchre alone holds the soul unimpaired.

VI

'Tis strange earth and water gender rage and surfeit;
Man has never been shriven by the Flood.
Melancholy is water in the skull of Saul;
Thought and sickness are pool and fen,
Words are drowned in the shallow eyes.
The knees are feeble coneys in the rain,
The hands are sedge and the plant of Cain.
Sorrow comes from river-vapor
Which reaps the caterpillar and the holm-oak maggot;
Clouds drain the loins but hearten the fungus;
And the moist wart on the fig descends to the feet.
Memory has the voice of the mussel;
The eye can scarce reflect
The aged mother's fumbling features;
But ravines and moribund hills
Singing as sea-valves in the morning
Recollect their parent Ocean.
The mind is torn by mock and conscience,

Mulcted as the silver-fir by the scantiest gale.
Memory affects the virgin cestus;
Affections are corrupt and friends are wandering water;
But the mastabah-tomb of rosy Syene granite
Is hard to quench.

VII

Grief is water and mother, but truth is stone.
There are wastes in men only granite can know.
God stood upon Mount Horeb, sterile rock;
The wilderness of *Sin* and *Paran* was Mosaic fate.
Rocks are for patience,
But dust is in diverse places
Gathering rage and derision.

Expired mountains suckle marble pillars;
Diorite is steadfast and starves the jackal.
The unguents of Astarte do not confuse Theban limestone;
Gall and the palmer-worm cannot be mummified,
And blood is no tablet for oaths·
The corridors of the pyramids are dry and constant,
Wicked Cheops in his tomb is psalm and awe,
All else is rheum and water·
Denial empowers the intellect, but repels the vulture.
Metaphysics is the immutable lament of porphyry,
Philosophy is the rigid plaint of stone.
Lineage thrives beneath the limestone hills;
The Nubian rock is the tablet of Cush.
The kings of Sidon quarried their tombs in Egypt,
And the steatite scarab remembers the Hyksos prince.
Angels are hieroglyphs cut into basalt ranges.

Rains breed the wanton lizard and dissolve filial love;
Moisture is the substance of the spider.
Sun and sphinx strike the maggot.

A scarab of feldspar is one of the Apostles,
Doubt is the pith of mountain alum,
Nitre and sterile chasm heal the void.
Humus is the manger of veins of garnet.
Jasper, agate and amethyst are gems of Eden;
Dearth was the ore of Adam's suffering mind.

Denial is bone of dragon and phoenix.
Not Canaan but Mount Nebo is Moses.
The most wearied peaks are Nahum and Isaiah,
The flowerless gullet of a hummock is prophet Haggai,
Golgotha is the place of skull and thought.
The remains of John the Wilderness is sard,
Onyx keep Terah, father of Abraham, in Ur;
Beryl is the shroud of the precious Magdalene,
Hope is malachite in the abject chest.
The loadstone is the will of Elijah,
Topaz is the words of speech
Guarded by Thoth, Hermes and Death,
Fate is masonry of Jacinth and Elisha.
Do the rocks we tread upon bleed?
Can the Pleiads assuage the panther?
Are the constellations epitaphs in heaven?
Hipparchus has said we are derived from stars;
Would that veins were wrought of quartz,
And the eye of a constant ore.

VIII

Poor in memorials is the present race;
Sing the dirge of the male parent.
The Patriarch is the vow of the mountain·
Cinder all till nullity or origin be fire and father·

Of the seed of fig is wild Edom,
Of the image of God is man.
The skull of Ham is Afric's shame,
Egypt is Mizraim, mentor of Homer, Musæus and Apollo.
The quince of the mild lowlands bears a malefactor;
Jacob is the olive of Judea,
But the stone of the fruit is ravening Benjamin.
Jacob is the apple of Haran, but the issue is Reuben.
Cant and self-love are the remnants of Jacob.
The almond of Galilee is Joseph, but Ephraim is the son.
The first issue of Adam was stones.
The father cannot seed his own image.
Adam was potherb and wild grass,
No decay skulked in cockle or the primal sorb;
Eve is moist and sin is round,
The deity casts his javelin at Leo,
When the dogstar parches the mandrake.
Vice and rage are vines of earth and water.
The four winds prowl through the head of Adam,
Sowing fitch, rape-broom and primal madness,
For Eve has torn Seth from his eye and flesh.
Feeble is the father who plants damage and pride
In her perfidious matrix;
Filial vows be done, the fathers dodder in the rains;
At Thebes the ancestral mummies were broken for fuel;
Sit on the ground where a thousand fathers took their rest.

IX

Adage is the dust of the sarcophagus;
Sin and love are mathematic in the tomb.
Trees sicken, and dying flowers offend,
Though asphodels remain the same in the meads of the dead.
What lives is sin and dross save it die;
There is no hurt in the winding-sheet.

Quarry the blood as old debris and mound,
Rubble and brick hide Rehoboth and Akkad;
Ruin is false morsel of fear and worm;
A body laden with Arabic mumia is a cure
For our sloven days of shame and Sodom.
Can the shroud of Thothmes betray the maggot?
Will the peristyle cower before Scythian Vulturnus?
The pectoral set in the skeletal breast is obsidian,
Papyrus is the vegetable raiment of queen Hentmehit;
A senile column at Persepolis is the eagle's perch;
The parched gazelle sleeps on pylons in the dunes.
Desert and skull prove the tooth of doubt;
Blood is king of lust,
But relic and chagrin are sayings and lore.
The grave of Daniel lies at Shus,
Water and pulse were his vision and table;
Rock shield him from his foe the palmer-worm;
At Abydos the head of Osiris lies alone.
The head of Paul was found in a sheepcote.
Bastion the remains of Zephaniah with sherd of Nineveh;
The lamentation of Jeremiah is pyrite,
May his tomb in Samaria never have one seam.
Hew the slab fresh with grief from the mountain,
The cave of Macphelah keep Abraham entire;

Loan not holy Isaac to the usurious worm.
Oil of cedar protect the haunches of Phut;
The body of Peter was laden with honey,
The ink of Hermes was steeped in galls.
Cyrus is a sage in his valley grave;
Nobel and vain are the craniums of David and Isaiah;
The sepulchres of Esther and Mordecai heal Ecbatna.
A prayer for the detritus of deceased Heliopolis
That contained the feet of Asenath, Joseph's bride.
What sacral rubble holds the tunic of Moses?
Is there yet a jamb or lintel Plato touched?
The burial urn expels the mad Erinyes,
Papyrus does not moulder in the mummy-pit,
Barley and corn-seed wax fat by dead Pharaoh;
A dried pomegranate is as entire as the prophet Samuel.
Sun and moon are potsherds in the Valley of the Tombs;
Rā and ancient Isis sleep among the tombed flowers.
Apostle Thomas is interred in Edessa,
King Tchesser is a litter of Egyptian glyphs,
He hewed his woe in a channel of rock.
Buttress all mortal works in calcareous stone,
Vilest Cambyses is an admonitory inscription.
Granite sustain Baal Peor and the winged Bull of Asshur,
Senmut wrought a coffin in the season of deceit.
The rocks of Hetnub are steadfast sons;
To betray is nature, fealty is in the grave.
Keep the bones and boast of Nimrod in gypsum;
Ignorance pours out the strength of awe.
The honey of Babylon succors Alexander;
The cere-cloth of Amenhotep is the stole of Osiris.
Where are the remains of Magog and the river Goshen?
The necropolis at Memphis can never be filled.
All annals are writ in equal dust.

Steep the body of Jacob in natron;
Lazarus is mouldy without the nard and drugs of Gaza;
Bitumen preserve the skeleton of Adam;
Cassia and myrrh guard the father's knees:
Sear the intellect with nitre and wormwood.
Osiris is prudent in a hundred sacred ossuaries;
Sorrow for the dead is olden skill.
The ancient gods taught Anubis embalming,
Hermes' sandals are shod by cobblers in Orcus;
Heed no sighs except the epitaph of stone,
Seasoned grief is the pith of the tomb.
A thousand slabs are more prophetic than Tiresias.

X

The portion of the mind is ten thousand wounds;
Memphis and Elephantine are my lineage,
Each ancient pillar is my holy father,
My mother is a derelict stone of ON,
The demise of olden sites is affliction,
An interred town in Ethiopia is my sin.
My brother is the dust of Pithom
Where Joseph fell upon the neck of Jacob.
Ruins and shambles of pylons are my kin.
Why are these rams and sphinxes out of season?
The massy pyramids die first at their summits;
The head is flesh for the eagle.
Thought is born before the cock crows,
Awe is thrice denied by the Apostle Peter.
The odor of daybreak is the meditation of Enoch.
Can salt and honey and prayer conquer Void?
The fungus sires its own noxious roots.

My footsteps gather chaff and bodings of the end.
I am the lackey of the worm,
The minion of sorrow and a menial of the dust.
Every door is the cormorant,
And solitude is my harp of sorrow.

XI

Ocean built the cities of Father Adam;
Byblos was a watery reed,
Uz was the potsherd of Job,
Erech a city of Amorite bricks,
Colchis was a trader in linen,
Panopolis cut stone for Anubis.
The body of Eridu was earthen Ea;
The dust of ON contains the thought of Moses.
The girdles of Bashan were fragrant with lore;
Women founded Carthage and the widow's purse,
Canopus and Memphis were her Tyrian petticoat,
Persepolis was her stibium-pot;
Ashkelon, Gath and Gaza were a college for whores.
Sidon and Arvad were the wanton beds of Ephraim.
Shurrupak, the garden of Sumer, was the gravel of sin.
Gilead, Larsa and Rehoboth were the works of the eagle,
Their broken temples and remnant gods its prey;
Babel and Calneh were fastened to Nimrod's latchet.
The idols of Borsippa sack the cunning bones.
Sippar was the tooth of the tiger,
Nineveh was the jaw of the lion,
Akkad the gazelle in the desert:
Pray for mighty Thebes, one obelisk is left.

XII

God shrive the artisans, Tubal-Cain, Gale and Garge,
Patriarchs of the tambourine, corn-grinder and ax.
James, brother of Jesus, was struck by a fuller:
Wool, linen, silk and cotton decay forever.
Apostles and Lazarus purge the vile, new house;
The sofa is as torpid as drunken Nabal,
The upholstery is obese with the maggots of Herod,
The bricks are cant, the wood mock poplar,
The window is a bearer of false witness.
Of plain gopher wood was the ark of Noah,
The idols the child Abraham vended were shaped of mud.
Joseph the carpenter fetch Lebanon cedar for the roof,
Jesus make ox-goads for the yard without the stall;
Noah is the quiet and contentment of the hands.

XIII

The first parent of knowledge was Adam,
And Eden was metaphysic,
But the word was invented by Cain.
Malice is the tongue of Cain that slew Abel.
The four rivers of Paradise
Are love, justice, peace and charity;
The Tree of Good and Evil is the intellect,
But the tree no man can touch is God.

The bedrock of the mind is chalcedony, onyx and rubies,
But knowledge without the passions of Abel is Cain.
Craft, without fire, water and stone,
Which are the love of one's brother, is Cain.

The tool genders envy, self-love and Cain.
An iron mace, an Ethiopic knife are boast and murder;
The eagle's talons covet the fingers of the potter,
Greed of belly and head double mortal hands;
Avarice, a tumor more dire than Iscariot, is Cain;
The hands bereft of glens and daybreak is Cain;
The foot that has trod olden places without a sigh is Cain.
Water, fire, earth, and air are Love and Abel.
Meditation, void of the hills and vales,
Which is tender recollection, is Cain.
Strength, without morning and evening quiet,
That are prayer, is Cain.
The first is last is creed and nature.
Alpha is Zeus, fatal Hermes, and Cain.
Man together is Abel, and apart he is Cain,
For Abel is the kin of every broken hope,
And the blood that flows in a single vein.
The vows lie beneath the pecking rains,
December is lament,
Twigs and green are summer's ruse,
The swallow and robin laugh,
And Cain forgets Adam's bones.
Guard the dead lest all be Cain.

XIV

Man of earth and water are sundered and perplexed.
Fish and man are Dagon, the Obelisk is Baal.
The Tree of Knowledge is the accursed Serpent,
And who eats of it creeps in the dust forever:
His head shall not be honest with his foot,
And his hands shall be cherub and raven;

His tongue shall be confusion, fox and shame;
He shall be perverse as Isaiah and Balaam
Who flogged the ass that saw the Angel.
Mischance and the vulture are constant,
Pleasant tidings drink the pity in mortals.

XV

The blood is the hunter of the human race,
And the venal tooth of Laban,
Penury and appetite plague it so it seems affection.
Vanity is an eagle that rends the head;
Self-love is the claw of the pard;
Must man weigh his words until the tomb?
The prophet is ashes and scorn in the world.
The lips if savory are a Buddha,
The teeth if not fangs are the smile of the Ephesian sod;
The neck when not the braggart of the lion
Is to be embraced.
Will all be chaff in the winds?

More towns and cities are destroyed by sexual disorders than by plagues, famine, and disease. Unless men follow some discipline they are demented from birth until their demise.

Man is not by nature ascetic or domestic; the human anthropoid would be a house-dove feeding on masts and roosting in the beeches were he not insane. Cyclops is a steadfast eater of men; the rough Solymi are incessantly arrogant; Ares or a javelin is the deity of Magog. It is the irregular outbreaks of passions that are the unexpected tyrants we seldom overwhelm. The fool is wet and parched, beckons one from whom he flees, and is cloyed, all in one hour. The hardest man to endure is one's self, and he is the most untrustworthy of foes. If one wears the livery of the meek, he crouches too low, or when one cries out, "My God, my God, I am a gnat," he dilates his throat; the recluse complains because the daughters of Judah do not come to gladden him.

Scylla is a fit of spleen which men must try to avoid, as we should endeavor to shun every tumid emotion, wrath, libidinous vision, cupidity, vanity, and self-love. Antisthenes was reported to have said that if the wise man does anything he does it in accordance with virtue as a whole.

Men with the fewest words break out on a sudden, and without cause; like Ajax they mistake the sheep for Agamemnon, or, as Achilles, go into combat with the River Scamander. Achilles, whose mother, Thetis, is hoary seawater, has cold wrath.

Man is the most confused beast in the earth; he marvels at the twelve houses of lust Tiberius built at Capri, and is unable to abhor Heliogabalus, who kept the snows of Armenia in diverse caves to cool his debauched Roman blankets. Alexander was embalmed in honey, and so are all his acts, because men care more for prodigies than they do for the wise or the just.

Human beings crave to be plants, shrubs, bog-moss, for their hearts cry out for quiet. The ordinary man dungs upon his spirit, and there is no nitre to cleanse him. Chagrin is the honey and the teacher; never to fail is a ditch and a delusion. We endeavor to be abstemious, but never slough a single folly. Vice is constant and ripens with age; old mulled sins are the worst.

Parmenides denied the existence of motion which is Eros, for whenever men move they stir up the blood. Augustus required his wife, Liva, to procure women for him because it was too painful for him on occasion not to discharge his distended vessels.

Human flesh is more ill-made than the quadrupeds in many respects. Goaded sorely and torn by his appetites, man envies the goat, who is able to have sexual intercourse all his life. He has the utmost desire to abstain from venery so long as he is capable of enjoying it. Origen deliberately became a spado because he knew that as long as man is tormented by that wallet of shame he will lie and cozen and scratch himself.

Seneca was of the mind that the groans and ejaculations that men fear and tremble for are in themselves trivial and contemptible. Not everyone is Demetrius, the Cynic, who was said by his adversaries to practice mortification. Epicurus, whose name has come to stand for Hedonism, took his sickness as a philosophic discipline, and though he died of the agony of the stone, he expired blessing his fate.

There is no doubt that sensuality is very attractive, and

it would be wrong not to set before the reader Lais of Corinth and the Pramnian wine. One cannot hide the pears, the fair Corinthian girls, and hope to inculcate in men a valorous continence. Everybody has to choose, and no one will honor a man who abstains from a vice of which he has no need, nor a teacher who feigns that pleasure does not exist.

But what is the good of being Solomon or Aristotle, and composing Ecclesiastes or the *Metaphysics*, if one turns his face to the wall because his penis was not erect in the presence of a chit. If man can make the wisest philosophy, and have no satisfaction of it because the pudendum is faithless, then all is lost, and man has no other choice but to be a sparrow or a newt. Nobody recollects pleasure except dimly, for one can remember the shape of a cube or an isosceles triangle, but not the color of the nipples of Daphne, nor the aches she once gave him.

Asceticism has always attracted the most carnivorous and sexual men. The Socratic head looked like neither the beautiful occiput of Apollo nor that of Buddha. Socrates was a thick-looking man, with the heavy mouth of an orgiast and the skull of Silenus. Want, Poverty, and Philosophy are such teachers that those who follow these three are often far better than men who appear to have the self-abnegating mien. Poverty is an Angel and the guardian of vision.

The young should be nurtured in Sparta, and they should be taught to meditate very often, for the navel is no more than the span of a palm from the shameful organ. A rude and hard infancy, according to Balzac, is best for the development of character. Eros is wily, feigning that the whole of human existence can be contained in the table, stool, and bed. There are many things to be said for the bed, provided one does not lie in it all day long; though Zeus could do it with impunity, man cannot. Besides, if a man is not a sen-

99

sualist, he is not likely to weaken the members he covets so that by forty they are a pendulous memorial of quondam pleasures.

"But in every case we must be most upon our guard against what is pleasant, and pleasure," Aristotle writes. Plato said that extreme pleasures and pains produce madness. Delights make men rave, and Tantalus is as greedy in Tartarus as in his days in the sun, for he never ceases to reach for the fruits the winds blow away from his voluptuous mouth. No one knows anything, and one can only surmise that his knowledge is no more than the rock of Sisyphus which rolls down from the peaks each day.

The men that are most interesting are those who have resisted the delights for which they ached. Solomon said, "Do not give all your strength to women," which is wise. One does not go to genius to be one of the cripples or the blind at Bethesda, but to be healed and to be seamed together again. The Essenes were craftsmen and healers, and the word means to cure. Luke was also a physician. A philosopher is a vestal when he rejects what hotly draws him. No matter what sage or philosopher or poet we cite we have to return to the same vexing dilemma, should man copulate?

It is hard to be Socrates when one has capital testicles, and only mimicry if one has not. Who can boast of the goodness of a dead phallus? And what bravery is there in the abstemiousness of a man who has a worthless prepuce? Moreover, it is redundant to be temperate if one is already impotent. What is overcome is good, for man has a negative conscience, the monitor or daemon in Socrates which prevented him from doing wrong, but did not compel him to perform what is right.

It is base to cocker vice, but we grow narrow and pithless if we are furtive about it, for this is at best a pretence, and the sage knows good and evil are kindred. The worst of men harm others, and the best injure only themselves.

Man is always tempted, and it is what he avoids rather than what he does that ennobles his character. The Crees knotted a few willow branches together which represented their deity, Kepoochikawn. This is a very rude image of a divinity, but less woe and vanity will come of it than from the Zeus of Praxiteles, or the temple of Solomon. Cree warriors ate live coals to be gods, and when they suffered pains, drums were beat so that their groans would not be heard.

It is possible to overvalue the ascetic habits, and many will complain that the beast's skin and club of Hercules, Stoic symbols for virtue and frugality, are not sufficient for their wit or manners. There is much confusion abroad, and our poets are no wiser than street-urchins. This, of course, Plato discerned, and many blame him for setting up a republic that is so austere . There is no man who is not a far greater despot to himself than he believes the laws of Plato's *Republic* to be.

Here is a riddle: if the gospel, and many wise books, have been written to govern the genitals, and to take away the imperial mind from this rugose pouch of mirth, how is it that a boy just growing his pubes, and while at chapel and without the least thought of anything save Mark and Luke, has an erection. This is as much of an enigma as the Ephesian sod, and must be considered along with the lilies and the Proverbs of Solomon.

Words are lies, but the testes are never hypocrites. The presbyters of the church and society do all they can to paralyze the pudendum, but desire is involuntary, and men go everywhere for no other cause than that they have tepid scroti or tumid ones.

It is harder to be indifferent to women than it is to be

101

courageous at Thermopylae or at Shiloh. Their habiliments trouble us sorely; were women naked, Aphrodite would have far less influence upon the lives of men. For this reason a savage Indian considers a nude female of no more worth than a needle, an axe or a shirt. Soon as Eve or Naamah, which in Hebrew signifies pleasure, covered her nipples and wore a girdle, men went to war, the heart was gorged with malice, and nobody could be quiet.

Man is willing to relinquish his friends, mortgage his farms, his pastures, glens, friths and all of Neptune's vasty surge to poke his nose through a placket. He is in Mahomet's Paradise when he can crawl like any mangy louse into a shirt-waist. How much human genius has been poured into the commonest sewer because man will lease, rent, borrow or inhabit any chink for an hour. St. Paul writes, "... The Flesh lusteth against the Spirit, and the Spirit against the Flesh."

Holofernes lost his life because the sandals that Judith was wearing deprived him of all his senses. Orpheus can tame mountain stones and the beasts of the woods more readily than he can pipe to that lawless, seminal cur which is the cause of most of man's woes. Kenneled and leashed within a pair of trousers he ranges the Kosmos no less than Lucifer. Everything that a woman does makes him draw up his ears and stand at attention. He is rapturous when he sees the greasiest dish-clout provided it is fastened to the bodice of any kitchen-scullion. Every article of apparel of a female is a terrible aphrodisiac to him, on or off her body. A comb, crisping-pin, wimple, a tire around her flocky hair, the sight of a gusset or the orient sound of her stays give him the most furious transports. Man, being dust, hungers not so much for his victuals, his joint of beef, trout and curds as he does for the hem of her dress, her toilet-water and per-

102

fumes; her skirt is the girdle around the earth.

Rapine is as old as the deluge; Lot sins with his two daughters because there were no men to go into them. The Word is corrupt when the earth is hindered. There will always be adultery, whoring, incest, and the practices of Venus Illegitima, the goddess of unnatural lusts, but expensive strumpets and the demolition of the bawdy-houses will bring about crimes not even the men at Sodom imagined.

He who is immune to the sweet baits of Eve is untrustworthy. It is as natural for women to bilk men as it is for the latter to spill the sperm into them. Casanova wrote: "I have through the whole of my life been the dupe of women."

We cherish Mary Magdalene no less than the immaculate Mary because the whore who can love is always a vestal. Such females never lose their purity. Every spring the goddess Hera bathed in cold, mountain water to recover her maidenhead, and anyone who does not believe this is utterly lacking in natural affection.

What can angel or man do with the heavens themselves when he is hungry for the thigh of a Shulamite? The hand is a roving, grazing animal, and crops the same meadows and pastures which satisfy the kine and the lambs of God. Panurge says, "Madame, know that I am so amorous of you, that I can neither piss nor dung for love."

It is impossible to be a philosopher or to understand literature when one has a penurious comprehension of human bodies. All knowledge, and what we call the intellect, is only the wisdom of the body.

We inherit our songs of lusts from angels. The heavens are also defiled, and God makes nothing that is not corrupt. The angel Azazel taught men the sweet uses of lechery; everything that lives is incontinent, the seas, the earth, the firmament; and the planets, are they not round and carnal?

Azazel invented cosmetics, buttons, adultery, incest and the hem-line of the skirt. Shamhai, the caitiff angel who seduced Ishtar, taught men to sleep, which is profligacy; he called man's attention to the teats, the toes, the fragrance of the terebinths, the joys of the oil trees, ilexes and showed the naked Canaanite women how to beautify their eyelids.

The Hebrew legends have it that it took the concupiscent angels nine days to fall from heaven to earth, though man can do it in three minutes. In spite of contrition, penance, humility, poverty, orisons, charity, and tears, which are Adam, Noah, Shem, Abraham, Isaac, Jacob and Job, man became more villainous. The more knowledge man had the more iniquitous he was; and, though the angels taught men how to plant, cut roots, recognize herbs, they did it in order to lie with their daughters, aunts, and sisters.

Men took every precaution to banish venery, foetid dreams, involuntary seminal nights, unlooked-for itches, scabs, phlegm, pustules, imposthumes, gibbering rafters and gibbous surfaces, objects and tools. He fell down, not seven times, but seven times seventy. He relied upon fumigation, Euclid, Kabalistic numerals to exorcise all the evil imaginings in his heart. It is told that Christ wore a seamless robe, for the simplest stitch is enough to make men lascivious.

The grum canting nations have seraphim, saints, martyrs, to protect them from the carnal contagion of doors, hinges, locks, keys, roofs, floors, walls, paper and books. They defy summer, spring, autumn and winter; when they see a pullet, a plover, a hen or a hypocritical swan which has the whitest feathers but the blackest flesh, they bleed at the nose or at the anus. No matter what they do they lament the fact that they did it, and they consult the sacred necrology of martyrs to fortify them. They empty whole missals of hymns and liturgies as though they were bedpans or close-stools. They know sin from alpha to omega, and whenever they smell lust they show the nose and nuzzle it. Who can guard man? According to St. Thomas, Seraphim, Cherubim, Throni, Dominationes, Virtute, Potestates, Principatus, Archangeli and Angeli are hampered in their frocks, sleeves and girdles all day long.

But who can closet his concupiscence in a frock, tunic, garment, or his sleeve? The fingers must have their joy of holding if only duckwood, sedge, or the ballock of a crane. What a saint or relic cannot accomplish satiety will. For after man has had his piece of flesh he will cry out for the alms of quiet. There is no viper so fierce as the soul, nor any adder deaf as too much spirit. The hart panteth after the waterbrooks, says my desire; "My God, my God, why hast thou forsaken me?" cries out my blood. Behold, a single ram is gelded by the horns in a sabek bush, but where is it? Take the lyre, play upon my sore and vexed thoughts; sound the timbrel, the sackbut, and dance unto my thirsting heart. I am the potsherd in the desert: O fill me with the pool of Heshbron. Sit by the waters of Dan, weep by the River Chebar, desire goeth not away until the tomb lies upon the head; for evil can never pass away.

No matter what man does he sins. Ham, like lust, extends from heaven unto the earth, going beyond the river Gihon, and toward Atel, which is the Atlantic, and travelling as far as Oceanus.

Behold, there are the spring rains, but the fresh leaves scatter the blood; the summer vines and grapes are as holy as God, but they vex the arteries; the south wind blows mild and the salt-surge fills the nostrils with infinite wonders, but the mouth loosely parts for the almond of desire. To withhold oneself from the glories of sea-kelp, the orchards and the grass is blasphemous. Cry unto the universe, spring up, O ye seeds, but it is thy peril and ruin.